THE NORTHERN COUNTIES TRAINING SCHOOL OF COOKERY

A COMPILATION

OF

Household Cookery Recipes.

PRICE NINEPENCE.

NEWCASTLE-UPON-TYNE
H. WARD AND SONS, WARD'S BUILDINGS, HIGH BRIDGE.
1913.

This volume was originally published in the United Kingdom
by H. Ward and Sons, Newcastle upon Tyne, in 1913

This facsimile edition published in the United States of America by
Diversions Books, an imprint of Diversions LLC
333 Jones Drive, Brandon, VT 05733, USA

In the United Kingdom and for all territories outside the USA and Canada:
Diversions Books division, Divine Art Limited
2, Lady Hamilton Drive, Swarland, Northumberland NE65 9HH, UK

This edition © 2014 Diversions LLC

All rights reserved. No part of this book may be reproduced or transmitted in any
form or by any means, electronic or mechanical, including photocopying, recording or
by any information storage and retrieval system without permission in writing from
the Publisher, except in the case of brief quotations embodied in critical articles or
reviews.

A Compilation of Household Cookery Recipes
ISBN: 978-0-9912232-1-3
Miss A. B. Rotherham, editor (original edition)
Library of Congress Control Number: 2014939782

diversions

Committee of Management.

Chairman—ALDERMAN SIR H. W. NEWTON, J.P.

Vice-Chairmen { REV. A. B. TEBB, C.C., J.P.
ALDERMAN SIR F. D. BLAKE, BART., D.L., J.P.

Appointed by the County Council of Durham:

MRS. J. G. GRADON.	MRS. WM. LATIMER.
ALDERMAN J. A. CURRY.	COUNCILLOR J. LOWES, J.P.
COUNCILLOR J. LAZENBY, J.P.	REV. A. B. TEBB, C.C., J.P.

MR. J. A. L. ROBSON (Consultative).

Appointed by the City and County Council of Newcastle-upon-Tyne:

ALDERMAN SIR H. W. NEWTON, J.P.	DR. ETHEL WILLIAMS.
,, SIR W. R. PLUMMER, J.P., D.C.L.	MRS. R. B. BRENTNALL.
MR. R. B. BRENTNALL.	MR. H. BENSON.

MR. SPURLEY HEY, B.A. (Consultative).

Appointed by the County Council of Northumberland:

MRS. M. I. RICHARDSON.	MISS E. PEASE.
ALDERMAN SIR F. D. BLAKE, BART., D.L., J.P.	ALDERMAN A. J. HAGGIE, J.P.
,, J. CROMIE, J.P.	COUNCILLOR A. E. BELL.

MR. C. WILLIAMS (Consultative).

PRINCIPAL—

MISS A. B. ROTHERAM.

SECRETARY—

THOS. C. MAJOR, 10, WEST STREET, GATESHEAD.

This compilation of Household Cookery Recipes has been prepared by the staff of the School for the use of students.

The School is recognised by the Board of Education as a Training School for Teachers of Cookery and Laundry Work, and is affiliated, for the purpose of certain examinations, to the National Union for the Education of Women in Domestic Science.

The courses are designed to meet the requirements of the following—

(1) Those of all classes who desire detached courses of practice lessons in Cookery, Laundry Work, Home Dressmaking Millinery, and Needlework, etc.

(2) Ladies to qualify for the Teachers' Full Diplomas in Cookery, Laundry Work, Dressmaking, Needlework, Millinery, Housewifery.

(3) Certificated Teachers in Elementary Schools, who wish to qualify for the Limited Diploma to teach Cookery under the Education Code.

(4) Girls and young women about to enter, or already engaged in domestic service.

(5) Classes are also arranged under the City and Guilds of London Institute for Certificates in Dressmaking and Millinery.

Orders are received for single dishes, or for entire luncheons, dinners, and suppers. Dishes sold at cost price.

The School is prepared to supply Lecturers and Teachers for courses of instruction in Elementary and other Schools, for County Council classes, for Girl's Friendly Societies, and Women's Clubs.

TIME TABLE OF CLASSES FOR OCCASIONAL STUDENTS.

A.—Cookery Practice Lessons.

Daily, from 10 a.m. till 1 p.m. (Saturdays excepted).

Fees (including use of material)—

I. Cottage	...	Ten Lessons, £1 5 0	Single Lesson,	3s. 0d.
II. Household	...	do. £1 10 0	do.	3s. 6d.
III. High-class	...	do. £2 2 0	do.	5s. 0d.

EVENING CLASSES, intended for Industrial Students, Half Fees.

Cookery Demonstrations.

Household, Mondays, 2 to 4 ... ... Ten Lessons, 4/6.
Single Lesson, 6d.
High-class, Wednesdays, 2 to 4 ... Ten Lessons, 8/6.
Single Lesson, 1/-.

B.—Laundry Work Practice Lessons.

Daily, from 10 till 1 and 2 till 4. Evening, 7 till 9.

Fees ... ... Six Lessons, 10/6. Single Lesson, 2/-.
Evening Students, Half Fees.

Laundry Demonstrations.

Wednesdays, 2 till 3·30. Ten Lessons, 4/6. Single Lesson, 6d.

C.—Dress Cutting and Dressmaking.

Daily, from 10·30 till 12·30 or 2 till 4. Evenings, 7 till 9.

Fees ... ... Twelve Lessons, 15/-. Evening Students, 5/-.

Practice Lessons in Tailor Cutting, Millinery, and Needlework by arrangement.

Occasional Students are admitted to the School for extended courses of instruction on special terms.

TRAINING FOR TEACHING DIPLOMAS IN

Cookery.
Laundry Work.
Housewifery, Dressmaking, Needlework, Millinery.

For course of instruction in these subjects see detailed Prospectus.

Detailed Prospectus and all information may be obtained from the Principal Miss A. B. Rotheram at the School.

Index.

	PAGE
STOCK:—	
Brown	7
Second	7
White	7
SOUPS:—	
Green Pea	8
Hare (Imitation)	8
Jenny Lind	9
Oxtail (Thick)	9
Kidney	10
Tomato	10
Tapioca Cream	10
Mulligatawny	11
Pea	11
Scotch Broth	11
FISH:—	
Fish Stock	12
Sole à la Maître d' Hotel	12
Sole à la Turque	12
Fillet Sole à la Turque	13
Cod (Boiled)	13
Fish Cakes	13
Plaice, Filleted	14
Sole au Gratin	14
Macaroni and Fish Pie	15
Steamed Fish	15
Croûtes of Fish	31
Fresh Herrings	34
Kedgeree	34
Spiced Mackerel	36
Potted Shrimps	38
MADE DISHES:—	
Beef Olives	16
Mutton Cutlets	17
Veal Cutlets	17
Durham Cutlets	18
Liver à la Française	18
Sheep's Head Baked	18
Haricot Mutton	19
Veal and Ham Pie	19
Galantine of Beef	20
Kromeskies	34
Raised Pie	59

	PAGE
ROAST MEAT:—	
Chicken	20
Pork, Sage Stuffing	22
Rabbit	22
Veal	24
BOILED MEAT:—	
Pressed Beef	24
Ox Tongue	25
Glaze	25
Ham	26
Chicken	26
Mutton	28
Rabbit	29
GRILLED MEAT:—	
Kidneys on Toast	30
Steak	30
Steak á la Maître d'Hotel	30
RE-HEATING OF COOKED MATERIAL:—	
Croûtes of Fish	31
Croûtes of Meat	31
Croquettes of Meat	32
Curry	32
Rissoles	32
Fricasee of Chicken or Veal	33
Meat or Fish Scallops	33
Kromeskies	34
BREAKFAST DISHES AND SAVOURIES:—	
Fresh Herrings	34
Kedgeree	34
Scotch Eggs	35
Anchovy Toast	36
Cheese Pudding	36
Savoury Omelet	36
Spiced Mackerel	36
Cheese Fondue	37
Macaroni Cheese	37
Potted Meat	37
Potted Shrimps	38
Curried Eggs	38

SAUCES:—

	PAGE
Shrimp	13
Brown	16
Bread	21
Apple	22
Piquante	23
Béchamel	26
Egg	26
Caper	27
Onion	28
Tomato	35
Horseradish	38
Mayonnaise	40
Jam	42
White	43
Custard	47
Marmalade	48

VEGETABLES AND SALADS:—

Mashed Potatoes	39
Potato Chips	39
Potato Croquettes	39
Salad	39
Boiled Artichokes	40
Stuffed Tomatoes	40
Celery and Sea Kale	41
Cauliflower au Gratin	41
French Beans	41
Carrot Mould	42

PUDDINGS:—

Castle	42
French Rice	43
Snowdon	43
Syrup	43
Apple Amber	44
Caramel Custards	44
French Pancakes	45
Semolina Soufflé	45
Apple Charlotte	46
Bread and Butter	46
Queen's Pudding	46
Chocolate	47
Lemon	47
Marmalade	47
Sweet Omelet	48

COLD SWEETS:—

	PAGE
Apple Jelly	49
Lemon Jelly	49
Lemon Sponge	50
Malvern Pudding	50
Prune Mould	50
Swiss Cream	50
Boiled Custard	51
Compôte of Oranges	51
Apricot Mould	52

CAKES:—

Girdle Cakes	52
Almond Cheese Cakes	53
Milk Rolls	53
Sally Luns	53
Cocoanut Buns	54
Shortbread	54
Swiss Roll	54
Fruit Cake	55
Shrewsbury Biscuits	55
Sponge Cake	55
Eccles Cakes	56
Soda Cake	56
Madeira Cake	57
Brandy Snaps	57
Lunch	57
Queen Cakes	57

PASTRY, ETC.:—

Cheese Straws	58
Lemon Cheesecakes	58
Raised Pie	59
Short Crust	59
Welsh Cheesecakes	59
Flaky	60
Rough Puff	60

INVALID:—

Cup of Cornflour	60
Arrowroot Pudding	61
Egg Jelly	61
Irish Moss Jelly	61
Chicken Panade	62
Chicken Broth	62
Egg Flip	62
Rice and Apple Snow	62
Mutton Broth	63

A COMPILATION OF

Household Cookery Recipes.

STOCK.

Stock (Brown).

Shin of Beef 1 lb.	Small Carrot 1.
Salt ½ teaspoonful	Small Onion 1.
Cold Water 2 pints.	Small Leek 1.
Peppercorns 3.	Celery 1 stalk.
Clove 1.	

Take the fat from the meat, and the marrow from the bone; cut the meat, and saw the bone into pieces. Put these into a saucepan, with salt and water. Bring gently to the boil. Skim. Prepare the vegetables. Cut them into *large* pieces. Stick the clove into the onion. Add these and the peppercorns to the saucepan. Simmer gently for three hours. Strain and cool. Take off the fat before using.

Stock (White).

Make in the same way as for brown stock, but use knuckle of veal instead of beef, and any other white meat as rabbit or fowl.

Stock (Second).

The pieces left from either brown or white stock, scraps of any cooked or uncooked lean meat or bone. Put these on in sufficient cold water to cover them, and simmer gently for five hours. Strain.

N.B.—Do not use the vegetables if they are soft, but add fresh ones.

SOUPS.

Green Pea Soup.

Pea Shells.		Green Pea (shelled)	½ pint.
Mint	1 sprig.	Sugar	1 lump.
Cold Water	3 pints.	Cornflour	½ tblspn.
Spinach	3 leaves.	Cold Water	1 tblspn.
Second Stock	1 quart.	Seasoning.	

Wash the shells and mint, put them in a saucepan with cold water. Boil 30 minutes or till tender; wash the spinach. Boil up the stock, add the peas, spinach, and sugar, and cook for 20 minutes, or till tender. Rub the peas through a hair sieve, drain the water off the shells, and rub these through also. Braid the cornflour with cold water and add; season; boil up and serve.

N.B.—If tinned peas are used, the mint must be boiled with them, and 12 spinach leaves used instead of 3.

Hare Soup (Imitation).

Gravy Beef	1 lb.	Thyme	1 sprig.
Onion	1.	Bay Leaf	1.
Butter	1 oz.	Peppercorns	4.
Flour	1 tablespoon.	Parsley	1 sprig.
Water or Stock	1 quart.	Cloves	2.
Small Carrot	1.	Mushroom Ketchup	2 tspns.
Turnip	1 small piece.	Worcester Sauce	1 tspn.

Cut the meat into small dice, flour them. Skin and cut up the onion; heat the butter; fry the meat; brown the onion and flour. Add the water or stock; prepare the vegetables; boil up the soup and skim. Add the rest of the ingredients; simmer gently 1½ hours; sieve. Add the ketchup and sauce, and forcemeat balls.

FORCEMEAT BALLS.

Stale Bread	1 tablespoonful.	Lemon Rind	a little.
Parsley	½ tablespoonful.	Salt.	
Suet	½ tablespoonful.	Pepper.	
Dried Herbs	1 teaspoonful.	Cayenne.	
Nutmeg	a little.	Egg	half one.

Prepare and mix all the ingredients and bind them together with the egg; make them into 12 small balls; flour them. If there is any fat on the soup take it off. Drop in the balls and simmer for 15 minutes.

Jenny Lind Soup.

White Stock	1 quart.	Egg Yolk	1.
Cornflour	½ oz.	Pepper.	
Milk	1 tablespoonful	Salt.	

Heat the stock. Braid the cornflour with the milk. Add it to the stock, stir and boil. Put the yolk into the tureen.

Pour the stock over the egg, stir vigorously. Season. Serve with bread fried in butter, and a little grated cheese.

FRIED BREAD.

Stale crumb of bread 2 ozs.   Butter   1 oz.

Heat the butter for three or four minutes. Skim it, pour it into a basin. Cut the bread into small dice. Pour the butter off the sediment into the frying pan. Heat it. Toss the bread in it, till it is a golden brown. Drain on soft paper, and dish on paper.

Oxtail Soup (Thick).

Oxtail	2 lbs.	Bay Leaves	2.
Cold Water	3 quarts.	Parsley	1 sprig.
Butter	1½ oz.	Thyme	1 sprig.
Carrot	1.	Cloves	3.
Turnip	1.	Stock	3 quarts.
Celery	3 stalks.	Butter	3 ozs.
Onion	1.	Flour	3 ozs.
Ham	2 oz.	Salt and Pepper.	

Separate the tail into joints; put them into a saucepan with sufficient cold water to cover. Bring it to the boil, and throw it away. Wipe and flour the joints. Heat 1½ oz. of butter, fry the joints and remove them. Prepare the vegetables. Cut up the ham, and fry these in the same butter as the joints. Put all in a saucepan with the stock, boil up and skim, add herbs and spice. Simmer 4 hours. Strain, and preserve the pieces of tail. When the stock is cold remove the fat. Heat 3 ozs. butter, add flour, brown it. Add stock, stir till it boils. Skim. Season. Add pieces of tail.

Tomato Soup.

Ham	1 oz.	Cold Water	1 tablespoonful.
Celery	1 stalk.	Stock	1 pint.
Onion (small)	1.	Cochineal	a few drops.
Carrot	1.	Tomatoes	1 lb.
Butter	½ oz.	Salt and Pepper.	
Cornflour	½ oz.	Bread.	

Prepare the ham, carrot, celery, and onion. Cut these up. Dissolve the butter in a saucepan, add the ham, celery, carrot, onion, cook a few minutes, but do not brown, and then add tomato; cook 20 minutes or till tender. Turn it on to a sieve. Place the stock in the same saucepan to heat. Rub the material on the sieve into the basin. Braid the cornflour with cold water. Add to it the stock, stir well and boil till it thickens. Add the purée and cochineal. Season. Re-heat.

Cut the bread in small dice, place them in a frying basket, and fry a light golden brown. Drain on soft paper. Serve on dish paper.

Kidney Soup.

Ox Kidney	½ lb.	Carrot, turnip, onion	1.
Lean Beef	¼ lb.	Celery	1 stalk.
Butter	1 oz.	Herbs	1 teaspn.
Flour	1 oz.	Water	1 quart.
	Seasoning.		

Heat the butter, fry the kidney and beef (cut into small pieces) till slightly brown, remove from pan. Brown vegetables and flour, add water, kidney, beef, herbs, and seasoning. Simmer 2 hours. Take out some of the kidney, rub the remainder through a sieve, re-heat, and serve with pieces of kidney in.

Tapioca Cream Soup.

White Stock (well flavoured)	1 pint.	Eggs	2 yolks.
		Milk	1 gill.
Crushed Tapioca	½ oz.	Seasoning.	

Put the stock on to boil, when boiling shake in the tapioca, and stir until cooked about 10 minutes. Beat the yolks and milk together, and strain into the soup, when it is just off boiling point, stir carefully until the eggs are cooked. Do not allow to boil after yolks are added.

Scotch Broth.

Neck of Mutton (scrag)	2 lbs.	Pearl Barley (blanched)	½ oz.
Water	2 qts.	Parsley (chopped)	
Carrot, Turnip, Onion	1.	dessertspoonful	1.
Celery	1 stick.	Seasoning.	

Remove all fat, and cut meat into small pieces. Put meat and bone into saucepan, add water and salt and bring to boil. Skim well, add vegetables (cut into small dice) and barley. Simmer 3 hours. Remove bone and some of the meat, add parsley, and serve.

Pea Soup.

Cold Water	4 quarts.	Celery	3 sticks.
Split Peas	1 pint.	Salt	1 teaspoonful.
Onions	2.	Pepper	½ ,,
Turnip	1.	Dried Mint	4 ,,
Carrot	1.	Cooked or uncooked ham bones.	

Soak the split peas for 12 hours and put them on in four quarts of cold water. Wash and cut the vegetables and when the water boils put them in with the peas; also, add the bones, salt, and pepper, and let it boil slowly for two hours, stirring occasionally. After that time take out the bones and rub the contents of the saucepan through a colander or sieve, re-heat and serve with dried mint and toast cut into dice.

Mulligatawny Soup.

Second Stock	2 pints.	Lemon Juice	2 teaspoonfuls.
Butter	1½ oz.	Flour	1¼ oz.
Carrot	1 small.	Curry Powder	½ oz.
Turnip	1 ,,	Rice	2 oz.
Apple	1 ,,	Herbs	1 bunch.
Onion	1.	Salt.	
Celery	2 sticks.		

Cut the vegetables and apple into small pieces. Melt the butter in a saucepan and put in the vegetables and apple, and fry for ten minutes without browning, mix the flour and curry powder together, and stir into the vegetables and cook a few minutes longer. Pour on the stock, add salt, lemon juice, and a small bunch of herbs, and boil slowly for 1½ hours. Pour through a fine strainer or hair sieve, re-heat and serve. Boiled rice should be handed round with this soup.

It is an improvement if this soup is made with chicken or mutton stock, and small pieces of the meat served in the soup.

FISH.

Fish Stock.

Water	½ pint.	Mace	1 blade.
Fish bones	2 oz.	Peppercorns	4.
Onion	1 *small* slice.	Salt.	

Place all in saucepan, simmer 10 minutes, strain and use for fish sauces.

Sole à la Maitre d'Hotel.

Sole	1.	Fish stock and milk	½ pint.
Butter	1 oz.	Parsley (chopped)	1½ tspn.
Flour	¾ oz.	Lemon juice	a few drops.

Wash and fillet sole, and fold the fillets neatly. Put on to a greased tin, add lemon juice, and sprinkle with pepper and salt. Cover with greased paper, so that no steam can escape. Next make fish stock with the bones.

Put the fish into a moderate oven and cook about 6 minutes. Make sauce. Take up the fish and arrange neatly on hot dish. Stir any liquor from the fish into the sauce. Pour sauce over fish and serve.

SAUCE.

Melt butter, add flour and mix well. Add fish stock and boil 4 minutes, add parsley and lemon juice, and seasoning if necessary.

Sole à la Turque.

Sole	1.	Shrimps	1 tablespoon.
Parsley (chopped)	1 teaspoon.	Herbs	¼ teaspoon.
Suet	¼ oz.	Butter.	¼ oz.
Breadcrumbs	2 teaspoon.	Browned bread-	
Pepper and salt.		crumbs	1 teaspoon.
Stock	¼ pint.		

Skin the sole both sides, cut off head, tail and fins, wash and dry. Cut down the centre of one side 1 inch from head and tail, raise the flesh from the bones, but do not remove it. Put the white crumbs, suet finely chopped, shrimps chopped, herbs, eschalot, parsley, pepper and salt, into a basin, and moisten with a little of the stock.

Insert the stuffing neatly under the fillet of sole, leaving the centre open. Put some pieces of butter on top, sprinkle over the fish with browned breadcrumbs, lay the fish on a greased dish, pour the stock round, and bake in a moderate oven 20 minutes.

The stock may be thickened, if liked, with 1 tablespoonful tomato sauce.

FILLETED SOLE À LA TURQUE.

The fish may be filleted instead of being left whole for a change.

Fish Cakes.

| Cooked Fish | ¼ lb. | Butter | ½ ounce. |
| Cooked Potatoes | 2 ounces. | Egg | 1 yolk. |

Seasoning:—Pepper and Salt.

Remove skin and bones from fish. Chop fish. Rub potatoes through wire sieve. Melt butter in saucepan, add fish and potatoes and put in the yolk. Season well with pepper and salt, and if too stiff add little milk. Mix over slow fire until mixture binds together. Turn on to plate to cool. Shape into small cakes. Egg and bread crumb, and fry in boiling fat. Drain on paper, and serve in pile on folded d'Oyley or paper. Garnish with fried parsley.

Any cooked fish may be used.

This mixture can be placed in pie dish, sprinkled over with crumbs, and baked in oven for 10 minutes.

Cod (Boiled).

| Water | To cover. | Vinegar | 2 teaspoonsful. |
| Cod | | Salt | 1 teaspoonful. |

Put the water on to get boiled. Scale the fish, trim, clean, weigh, and wash it. Add salt and vinegar to the water. Put in the fish, bring it to the boil, skim. Simmer for 10 minutes to the lb. and 10 minutes over, or until the flesh begins to leave the bone. Place on a hot dish.

PREPARE THE SHRIMP SAUCE.

Shrimps	¼ pint.	Flour	¾ oz.
Fish Stock	½ pint.	Anchovy Sauce	2 teaspoonsful.
Butter	1 oz.	Cayenne	

Wash the shrimps. Skin them. Put the skins with ½ pint of water to stew for stock; strain. Melt the butter in a saucepan; add the flour. Mix thoroughly; add the stock. Let it boil 3 or 4 minutes. Add the anchovy sauce, shrimps, and cayenne, and serve in tureen.

Remove the cod; drain it, and garnish with slices of lemon and parsley.

Sole au Gratin.

Sole	1	Lemon Juice	1 teaspn.
Onion	¼ teaspoon.	Cayenne.	
Parsley	1 teaspoon.	Salt	¼ teaspn.
Butter	½ oz.	Brown Crumbs.	
Mushrooms	2	Stock	3 tablespn.

The sole should be sent to table in the dish in which it is cooked. Skin, trim, and wash the fish. Skin the onion and cut it up. Wash the parsley; dry, and chop it and the mushrooms. Butter the dish with one-half of the butter. Sprinkle over the dish half of each of the ingredients, except bread crumbs. Lay the fish on this. Sprinkle over the fish the remainder of the ingredients. Cover it with browned bread crumbs; put the remainder of the butter over the surface in small pieces. Pour round the stock. Bake in a moderate oven for 15 or 20 minutes.

Sole or Plaice (Filleted) and Fried Parsley.

Plaice	1.	Bread Crumbs.	
Parsley.		Flour	1 teaspoonful.
Frying Fat.		Salt	1 saltspoonful.
Egg	1.	Pepper	¼ saltspoonful.

Wash the plaice. Cut the flesh down the middle line from head to tail; free the edges of the fish from the back bone. Cut the flesh off evenly. Keep the knife close to the under bone. Place skin side of the fillet downwards. Dip the finger and thumb in salt, hold the skin firmly, loosen the flesh at the tail, put the knife between the skin and flesh, draw the skin, pressing well on it, so that the knife separates the flesh from the skin. Wash the fillets and dry them. Roll them up in a cloth for some time. Wash some good sized pieces of parsley and dry them. Put the fat on to heat. Break an egg on a plate and beat it. Put bread crumbs in paper. Cut the fillets lengthwise, knot them, with the skin side inwards. Mix the flour, pepper, and salt. Draw the fillets one by one through this mixture. Remove them one by one to the egg. Coat them well, especially the edges. Lift them one by one into the crumbs. Lift the corners of the paper and toss the crumbs over. Remove from crumbs with the sides of the hands. Shake off the loose crumbs. Press on those that adhere. If the fat smokes, put 4 pieces of fish into the basket. Fry a light golden brown. Drain on soft paper. See that the fat smokes again. Fry the remainder of the fish. Put the basket back in the fat; throw in the parsley. When the hissing ceases, turn the parsley on to a sheet of paper. Lift this and move the parsley gently backwards and forwards. Dish the fish lightly on paper. Place the parsley in a heap in the centre.

Steamed Fish.

| Plaice | 1. | Butter | ¼ oz. |

Lemon juice, a few drops.

Put a saucepan of water on to boil. Fillet the fish, skin, wash, and dry it. Slightly butter 2 plates, double the fillets. Put them on one plate, squeeze over a few drops of lemon juice, cover with a second plate. Place the plates over the saucepan of boiling water. Steam from 10 to 15 minutes.

PREPARE THE WHITE SAUCE.

Egg	1.	Flour	¾ oz.
Parsley.		Milk and fish stock ½ pint.
Butter	1 oz.	Salt	a pinch.

Boil an egg hard. Wash and chop the parsley. Melt the butter in a saucepan. Add the flour. Stir in the milk. Boil for 5 minutes. Season. Stir in the liquor off the plates the fish was steamed on.

Halve the egg. Rub sufficient of the yoke through a sieve for decoration. Put the halved eggs in the centre of the dish, point upwards. Arrange the fillets round the egg. Pour the sauce over. Garnish the folded tips of each alternate fillet with chopped parsley and yolk of hard-boiled egg.

Macaroni and Fish Pie.

6 ozs. Cooked Fish.
2 ozs. Cooked Macaroni.
½ pint Fish Sauce.
2 tablespoonsful White Bread Crumbs.
½ oz. Butter.
Seasoning.

Break the fish and macaroni into small pieces and remove all bone and skin from the fish. Mix to this sufficient sauce to well moisten the mixture and season with salt and cayenne. Turn into a greased pie dish and cover over with the breadcrumbs. Put the butter on in small pieces. Bake in quick oven or in front of the fire until thoroughly hot through and a nice brown colour on top. Serve in the pie dish on a paper or table napkin folded.

MADE DISHES.

Beef Olives.

Rump Steak	1 lb.	Lemon rind (chopped)	1 strip.
Brown Sauce	¾ pint.	Seasoning.	
Crumbs of Bread	2 ozs.	Egg	½.
Suet	1 oz.	Worcester Sauce	2 teaspn.
Parsley	1 tblspn.	Potatoes (cooked)	6 ozs.
Thyme	1 teaspn.		

The steak should be lean, and ½ an inch thick. Put the brown sauce to warm in a stewpan. Trim the meat, divide it into strips 2 inches wide and 4 inches long. Flatten these with the knife. Prepare the bread, suet, parsley, thyme, and lemon rind for the forcemeat, season and bind with egg. Make the same number of portions of forcemeat as there are strips of meat. Spread one division on each strip. Roll up and tie with string. Put them into the sauce. Simmer gently 1½ hours. If the potatoes are cooked, warm them. Prepare the mashed potato, mould and place on a dish. Make it quite hot. Test the olives with a skewer; if they are tender, take them out, remove the string, and place the olives on the potato. Braid 1 teaspoonful of flour with the ketchup. If necessary, add a little stock. Add to the gravy, boil, and season. Pour the gravy over the olives. Wipe the edge of the dish with a warm cloth, and serve.

This can be varied by using veal and sausage meat.

Brown Sauce.

Good Second Stock ¾ pint.

Butter	1 oz.	Turnip (small)	
Flour	¾ oz.	Carrot	,,
Tomato	1	Onion	,,
Peppercorns	6	Thyme and Bay Leaf.	

Cut vegetables into small pieces and dry them. Melt the butter, and add vegetables and herbs. Fry until brown, add the flour and brown it. Add tomato and stock, and simmer for 15 to 20 minutes. Strain and use.

Mutton Cutlets.

Neck of Mutton	3 bones.	Egg	1.
Butter or Lard	2 ozs.	Salt.	
Bread Crumbs	¼ lb.	Pepper.	

The mutton must be cut from the best end of the neck. It should be *lean and small*.

If the potatoes are uncooked, boil and sieve them. If cooked, warm and sieve them.

Saw off the chine bone, and the end of the ribs. Separate the rib bones, and cut through the meat. Divide it into cutlets. They should be of the same thickness. Remove unnecessary fat. Scrape the bones. Place small pieces of bone in the cutlets that have none, and flatten the cutlets with a knife. Prepare the mashed potato, and mould it on a dish. Put it to heat. Break the egg on a plate, and beat it. Prepare the crumbs, and place them on paper. Season the cutlets, egg and crumb them. Put the butter into the sauté pan. When hot fry the cutlets for 10 minutes. Turn them once or twice. When golden brown, drain on soft paper, and dish. Pour gravy round the cutlets. Tomato or brown sauce may be used. Garnish with cooked vegetables.

Veal Cutlets.

Fillet of Veal, ¾-inch thick	1 lb.	1 Egg.	
Bacon, 1 small slice to each cutlet.		Parsley.	
		Thyme.	Mix together.
Lard	2 ozs.	Lemon Rind	
Tomato Sauce	½ pint.	Salt.	
		Pepper.	

Trim the meat. Cut into even-size pieces, round or oblong, 2 inches across. Flatten them with a knife. Prepare the bacon rolls in thin slices 2 inches wide and 4 inches long. Put them on a skewer in a tin.

Prepare bread crumbs; put them on paper. Break the egg on a plate, beat it, add the lemon, parsley, thyme, salt, and pepper. Put the bacon in the oven to cook. Egg and crumb each cutlet separately. Fry a golden brown, take them up and drain on soft paper. Dish them with a roll of bacon between each. Pour the tomato sauce round. Garnish with peas if liked.

Durham Cutlets.

Cooked Meat (minced)	¼ lb.	Stock or Milk	¼ pint.
Bread Crumbs	2 oz.	Egg	1
Parsley (chopped)	½ teaspn.	Mushroom Ketchup	1 teaspn.
Butter	½ oz.	Worcester Sauce	1 teaspn.
Flour	½ oz.	Salt, Pepper, Cayenne.	

Egg, Bread Crumbs, Frying Fat, Macaroni.

Make a panada with the butter, flour, and stock, add seasonings, meat and bread crumbs, parsley, sauces, and egg. Mix well, and spread evenly on a wet plate, set aside till firm. Divide into 8 triangular shaped pieces, flour the board and fingers, and shape into cutlets, egg and bread crumb, and fry a golden brown. Put an inch of macaroni into the narrow end, and serve hot on dish paper.

Liver à La Francaise.

Calf's Liver	1 lb.	Parsley (finely chopped)	1 teaspoonful.
Bacon	2 oz.	Worcester Sauce	1 dessertspoonful.
Breadcrumbs	4 tablespoonful.	Stock	½ pt.
Mushrooms (chopped)	3		
Onion (chopped)	½ teaspn.		

Salt, pepper, nutmeg, a little dripping, brown breadcrumbs.

Cut the liver into slices ½ an inch thick, put on greased tin, mix together the breadcrumbs, mushrooms, onion, parsley, and seasoning, sprinkle this over the slices of liver, and put on each a thin slice of bacon, pour round the stock, and cook in a moderate oven ¾ hour. Arrange the pieces of liver on a dish, add to the gravy the Worcester sauce, and pour round, sprinkle the brown breadcrumbs lightly over the bacon, and serve.

Baked Sheep's Head.

1 Sheep's Head and Pluck.		Carrot	1.
Water to cover.		Turnip	1.
Sprig of Parsley.		Onion	1.

SAUCE.

Butter	1 oz.	Mixed Herbs	¼ teaspnful.
Flour	1 oz.	Worcester Sauce	½ teaspnful.
Sheep's Head Stock	½ pint.	Anchovy Essence	½ teaspnful.

Savoury Crumbs.

Breadcrumbs	2 ozs.	Salt	½ teaspoonful.
Chopped Parsley	1 tablespoonful.	Pepper	¼ teaspoonful.
Egg	1.	Butter	½ oz.

Garnish—Brains.

Cleanse the head and place with the heart and half the liver in a saucepan. Cover with water and when boiling add the vegetables, and cook till meat is tender, about 1½ hours. Take up the head, liver, and heart. Remove the bones from the head and place it on a greased tin. Brush over with egg and cover thickly with savoury crumbs. Place small pieces of butter on top and bake in oven until a rich brown, 20 to 30 minutes. Cut the liver and heart into dice. Make the sauce, and put the dice into it.

Blanch the brains and cut into neat pieces.

Dish the head on a hot dish, pour the mince round, and garnish with the brains.

Veal and Ham Pie.

Fillet or lean Veal	1 lb.	Hard boiled Eggs	2.
Ham or Bacon	2 oz.	Pepper and Salt.	

Cut up the veal, ham, and eggs into pieces, and place in a pie dish in layers. Season each with pepper and salt, and half fill the pie dish with water, or stock made from the bone and trimmings of the veal. Cover the dish with rough puff or short crust pastry, decorate with the trimmings of pastry, brush over with well-beaten egg, and bake in quick oven at first and then cooler for about 2 hours.

Fill the pie with veal stock and serve on d'Oyley or dish paper.

Haricot Mutton.

Neck of Mutton	1 lb.	Dripping	1 oz.
Haricot Beans	1 tablespnful.	Flour	1 oz.
Onion	1.	Pepper and Salt.	
Turnip and Carrot	1.	Stock or Water	¾ pint.

Cut the onion into slices and fry in the dripping. Remove from the pan and fry the mutton on both sides. Take out the pieces of meat and stir in the flour, allowing it to brown in the dripping; stir in ¾ pint of water or stock and allow it to boil up. Put back the pieces of meat. Cut the carrot and turnip into dice; add the vegetables to the saucepan, season with pepper and salt to taste; skim well, move the saucepan to the side of the fire to simmer gently for about two hours. For serving, arrange the meat in a circle and the vegetables in the centre, and pour the gravy over.

Galantine of Beef.

Beef	1 lb.	Stock	1 gill.
Bacon	½ lb.	Whole Eggs.	2.
Bread Crumbs	6 oz.	Pepper and Salt.	

Pass the beef and bacon through a mincing machine, and put it into a basin with the bread crumbs and seasoning. Beat the eggs and stock together and pour them to the other ingredients, and mix well. Form into a short roll with the hands, tie in a pudding cloth, boil for 2½ hours, press between two dishes until cold, and then glaze on the top.

ROAST MEAT.

Chicken (Roast).

| Chicken | 1 | Bacon | 6 rolls. |
| | Flour. | | |

Pluck the bird, and remove the stems of feathers, cut off the head. Make an incision across the back of the neck, one inch from the body; slit the skin of the neck down the back to the incision, loosen the skin round the neck, cut the neck off at the root. Take out the crop; insert the finger at the neck, loosen the liver and other parts under the breast. Make an incision of one inch at the vent, put two fingers through, take hold of the gizzard and carefully draw out all the interior at once. Do not break the gall bladder. Look through the fowl from one end to the other, see that it is perfectly cleared out. Wipe the inside with a warm cloth. Clean the giblets (neck, heart, liver, and gizzard), soak the neck in warm salt and water. Remove the gall bladder from the liver. Cut the gizzard down the centre by the white line; be careful to cut only the first or outer skin. Draw off the outer skin, do not break the inside bag. Wash the giblets; use them to make stock for the gravy to be used with the roast chicken, or, if liked, a part of the gizzard and liver can be put in the wings. Singe the bird, scald the legs, and draw off the outer skin. Do not scrape them, remove the tips of the claws with a knife. Draw the neck skin over the opening, make a slit in the skin of the vent, put the parson's nose through this.

Place the tips of the pinions towards the backbone, let them press on the neck skin and hold it down. Place the chicken breast upwards; press the thighs into the sides, so as to raise the breast. Pass a trussing needle through the flesh, close to the second joint of the wing on the right side; continue it through the body to catch the same joints on the left side. Bring the string to the first joint of the wing on that side, pass it through the flesh at the back of the bird. Catch the tips of the pinions and the neck skin, go through the flesh near the first joints of the wing on the right side. Tie the two ends of the string together. Put the needle into the gristle on the right side, close to the parson's nose (leave an end of string), pass the trussing string over the right leg, through the skin at the bottom of the breast bone, over the left leg, through the gristle close to the parson's nose on the left side, carry it behind the legs, and tie firmly to the end of string left for the purpose.

Put the chicken on a stand in a baking tin. Cover the breast with a slice of fat bacon or some dripping. Bake ¾ hour to 1 hour. Baste often.

Prepare the Bread Sauce.

Onion	1.	Stale Crumb of Bread	1 oz.
Peppercorns	4.	Salt.	
Milk	½ pint.	Butter	½ oz

Put the ingredients into a saucepan and soak 5 minutes. Stir over slow fire for 10 or 15 minutes. Add more milk if too thick.

Prepare the bacon. Fifteen minutes before dishing remove bacon from breast of chicken, dredge the breast with flour, and froth it with frequent basting. Add rolls of bacon to the tin.

Remove the string from the chicken. Place the chicken on a hot dish. Pour the fat from the tin. Strain the giblet stock into the tin, stir well, and let it boil. Season. Pour a little of the gravy round the bird, serve the remainder in a tureen, and send bread sauce to table with it. Garnish with rolls of bacon.

Pork (Roast).

Leg or Loin of Pork.

Joint the meat. Wipe it with a damp cloth. Score it. Weigh, and allow at least 25 minutes to the pound, and 15 minutes over. Put the meat on a stand in a baking tin, and place in the hottest part of the oven, or hang in front of a very clear fire for the first five or ten minutes, then cook less quickly. Baste often.

Sage and Onion Stuffing.

Onions	2 boiled.	Bread Crumbs	1½ ozs.
Sage	7 leaves.	Butter	¾ oz.
Pepper and Salt.			

Peel and scald the onions and throw away the water. Boil the onions until quite tender, about 30 minutes. Scald the sage.

Chop the onions and sage finely, add the bread crumbs (which should be freshly made) and the butter. Season with pepper and salt, and use as stuffing for roast pork, goose or duck.

If preferred this stuffing may be turned into a well greased pie dish, baked separately, and served with the pork.

Prepare the Apple Sauce.

Sharp Juicy Apples ¼ lb.　|　Sugar to taste.

Peel the apples, core, and quarter them. Put into a jar or basin, cover, place in oven. Cook till tender. Beat well. Pour into a tureen, and serve hot.

When the joint is cooked, place on a hot dish, pour the dripping from the tin into a basin (add boiling water at once to the dripping to clarify it). Pour boiling water on to the brown particles in the pan, boil over the fire, stir well, pour round the joint. Serve with apple sauce.

Rabbit (Roast).

1 Rabbit.　|　6 Bacon Rolls.

If necessary, paunch the rabbit. Chop off the first joint of the legs. Loosen the skin at the stomach, draw it up to the back. Slip the hind legs out of the skin. Skin the tail. Pull the skin towards the head till the fore legs are reached. Slip the forelegs out of the skin. Use a knife to skin the head;

skin the ears; take out eyes. Draw away the heart, liver, and lungs; clean them and put in water to simmer. If there are many wounds, wash the rabbit, wipe the inside; stand the head to soak in a basin of warm salt water. Cut across the sinews under the legs. Make forcemeat.

FORCEMEAT.

Stale Bread	2 ozs.	Thyme	$\frac{1}{2}$ teaspoonful.
Suet	1 oz.	Salt.	
Parsley	1 tablespoon.	Pepper.	
Lemon Rind	1 strip.	Egg	$\frac{1}{4}$.

Prepare the bread, suet, parsley, thyme, and lemon rind. Season and bind with egg.

Stuff the body with this and sew it up. Draw the hind legs forward and the fore legs backwards till they overlap. Put the trussing needle through the two legs where they overlap (leave an end of string). Run the needle through the body to the opposite side, strike the point where the legs overlap. Pass the needle back again to the other side from a little above the fore leg joints. Tie the two ends of string. Run a skewer through the mouth, and fix the head firmly between the shoulders. Wrap the ears in greased paper. Place thick slices of bacon over the back. Put it on a stand in a baking tin. Place in a quick oven for a few minutes, then bake less quickly for $\frac{3}{4}$ hour. Baste it frequently. Prepare bacon rolls. Fifteen minutes before dishing remove the bacon from the back of the rabbit and the paper off the ears. Dredge flour over and baste. Add bacon rolls to the tin, cook them. Remove them. Draw the string and skewer from the rabbit. Place on a hot dish. Pour nearly all the fat from the tin. Stir 1 teaspoonful flour smoothly in; brown. Strain in the prepared stock, boil, season, colour. Garnish with rolls of bacon.

PIQUANTE SAUCE.

Vinegar	1 tablespoonful.	Mushroom	1.
Harvey Sauce	1 teaspoonful.	Bay leaf	1.
Stock	$\frac{1}{2}$ pint.	Onion and Carrot	small piece.
Butter	$\frac{3}{4}$ oz.	Flour	$\frac{1}{2}$ oz.

Seasoning.

Clean and cut up vegetables into small pieces, reduce them in the vinegar until vinegar is nearly dried up, and fry them brown in the butter, add flour and brown it. Stir in stock, bay leaf, Harvey sauce, and simmer 15 minutes. Strain and serve with cutlets or roast rabbit.

Veal (Roast).

Fillet or Breast	2 lb.	Lemon Rind	1 strip.
Stale Crumb of Bread	2 ozs.	Salt.	
Marrow or Suet	1 oz.	Pepper.	
Parsley	1 tblspn.	Egg	$\frac{1}{4}$.
Thyme	$\frac{1}{2}$ tspn.	Bacon	2 oz.

Remove the bones, put them on to simmer. Prepare the bread, suet, parsley, thyme, and lemon rind for the forcemeat; season and bind with egg. If breast is used, flatten the meat and spread the forcemeat over. If fillet is used, place forcemeat in the hole, left by the bone. Bind the joint round with tape, cover with the caul. If there is none, spread the lean part of the fillet with dripping. Place on a stand in a tin, put in a quick oven for 5 minutes; turn it, and bake less quickly for about $1\frac{1}{2}$ hours. Cut rolls of bacon, run a skewer through them. Fifteen minutes before dishing, dredge the veal with flour; baste well. Add the rolls of bacon to the tin.

GRAVY.

Butter	$\frac{1}{4}$ oz.	Stock	$\frac{1}{2}$ pint.
Flour	$\frac{1}{4}$ oz.	Browning.	

Melt the butter in a saucepan, stir in the flour. Strain in the stock; stir and boil.

Take the veal and bacon from the tin. Remove the tape. Place the veal on a hot dish. Pour off the fat. Pour in the boiling sauce. Boil. If necessary, add browning. Pour a little gravy round the joint. Garnish with bacon and slices of lemon. Serve the remainder of gravy in a tureen.

BOILED MEAT.

Tongue or Pressed Beef.

Thick Ribs Beef, 4 lbs; or Tongue, 1.

PICKLE.

Bay salt	$3\frac{1}{2}$ lbs.	Saltpetre	$2\frac{1}{2}$ ozs.
Porto Rica sugar	2 lbs.	Whole black peppercorns	2 ozs.
Whole mixed spice	2 ozs.	Water	2 gallons.

Failing Bay salt, use 5 lbs. common salt.

Method for making Pickle.

Put all the ingredients into a pan, and boil for ½ hour. Strain into a jar, and when *quite cold* put in meat, tongues, etc., and leave in 7 days. For a large piece (14 or 15 lbs.) the usual time for pickling is one day to each lb. The meat should be turned in pickle when it has been in half the time.

Take out of pickle and stew gently with the following:—

Sufficient warm water to cover the meat.		Allspice	1.
		Leek	1.
Carrot	1.	Celery	1 stalk.
Turnip	1.	Peppercorns	2.
Onion	1.		

Put the meat into the water, bring it to the boil. Skim. Prepare the vegetables, add them to the meat. Let all simmer 2½ hours, or till tender. Lift out the meat; remove the bones, tie round with tape. Press, and leave till cold. Then trim and glaze it.

To Boil an Ox Tongue.

A pickled tongue should be soaked for 2 or 3 hours in cold water. Then put on to boil in warm water with a bunch of savoury herbs. Let it come slowly to the boil, skim well, and simmer slowly for about 3 hours after coming to the boil. When cooked plunge it into cold water, so that it will skin more easily, which must be done carefully, especially at the tip of the tongue. When skinned set the tongue with the root end against a board or wall, fasten into position by placing a fork through the root and another through the tip of the tongue into the board, keeping it well arched, so that it will stand well. When quite cold, trim off the roots. Glaze (see page 29) it well, put a rouche round the root, and garnish with parsley.

NOTE.—TO SERVE HOT.

The tongue should be wrapped in buttered paper, and made hot in boiling water for ½ hour; then glazed and garnished with tufts of cauliflower or Brussels sprouts, and served with tomato, piquante, or poivrade sauce.

Meat Glaze. No. 1.

Strong Jelly Stock	1 quart.	Cold Water	¼ pint.

Remove all fat from the stock, melt the stock and strain it through muslin. Put it back into the saucepan, and when boiling add the cold water to clarify the stock. Boil quickly, skimming away carefully any scum as it rises; when the stock takes a syrupy consistence it is done. Pour into jar and keep.

This can be made in large quantities when there is spare stock to use, as it will keep any length of time if covered with lard after it is set in the jars.

Quickly Made Glaze. No. 2.

Clear Stock or Water	½ pint.	Tomato Puree	2 tablspn.
Gelatine	¾ oz.	Sherry	2 tablspn.
Leibig	2 teasp.		

Carmine or browning to colour.

Put all the ingredients into a clean saucepan and stir until melted. Boil very quickly until it forms a glaze as above, and then use.

To Boil a Ham.

Select a nice ham, and soak for 24 hours in cold water. Scrape and clean well, put on to boil in warm water, and allow to simmer steadily for 3 hours. Allow it to get cold in the water, then take out and remove the rind, trim the surface smoothly with a knife, and place on a baking sheet in the oven for a few minutes, then dry well with a clean cloth to absorb the grease. Sprinkle with finely-made browned bread crumbs.

Place a frill round the knuckle bone, and garnish with parsley.

NOTE.—A ham of 12 to 14 lbs. weight takes about 4 hours to cook.

The ham may be glazed and decorated with forced butter.

Chicken (Boiled).

White Stock or Water	1 quart.	Clarified Fat	½ oz.
Chicken	1.	Lemon Juice	Few drops.

Put the stock or water on to heat.

Pluck the bird and remove the stems of feathers, cut off the head. Make an incision across the back of the neck, one inch from the body. Slit the skin of the neck down the back to this incision. Loosen the skin round the neck. Cut the neck off at the root, take out the crop. Insert the fingers at the neck, loosen the liver and other parts under the breast. Make an incision of one inch at the vent, put two fingers through. Take hold of the gizzard, and carefully draw out all the interior at once. Do not break the gall bladder. Look through the chicken from one end to the other, see that it is perfectly cleared out. Wipe the inside with a warm cloth. Clean the giblets (neck, heart, liver, and gizzard). Soak the neck in warm salt water. Remove the gall bladder from the liver. Cut the gizzard down the centre by the white line, be careful to cut only the first or outer skin, draw off the outer skin, do not break the inside bag. Singe the bird, cut the skin round the first joint of the legs. Pull the joints to draw out the sinews of the thighs. Insert a finger and loosen the skin all round the thighs, push the drumstick upwards until it slips under the breast skin. Put the parson's nose inside the body. Draw the neck skin over the opening. Place the tips of pinions towards the backbone, let them press on the neck skin and hold it down. Place the chicken breast upwards, press the thighs into the sides, so as to raise the breast. Pass a trussing needle through the flesh close to the second joint of the wing on the right side (leave an end of string). Continue it through the body and catch the same points on the left side. Bring the string to the first joint of the wing on that side, pass it through the flesh at the back of the bird, catch the tips of the pinions and the neck skin; go through the flesh near the first joint of the wing, on the right side; tie the two ends of the string together.

Put the needle into the gristle on the right side close to the parson's nose (leave an end of string). Pass the trussing string over the ends of the drumsticks, catch it into the gristle on the left side, pass the string through the body close to the backbone; tie the ends together. Squeeze a few drops of lemon juice over the breast. Grease the paper. Tie the chicken up in it. Put it into boiling stock or water, and simmer for 1 to 1½ hours. Remove the paper and string from the chicken, place it on a hot dish, pour the sauce over. Hold the sieve or strainer over the breast and rub through the hard-boiled yolk of an egg.

Send boiled ham, tongue, or bacon rolls to table with it.

Serve with Bechamel or egg sauce.

Egg Sauce.

Boiling Water.		Milk	½ pint.
Eggs	2.	Cayenne.	
Butter	1 oz.	Salt.	
Flour	¾ oz.	Lemon Juice	Few drops.

Put the eggs into boiling water and boil for 13 minutes. Melt the butter, stir in the flour, add the milk, stir and boil, season, simmer for 5 minutes. Crack the eggs and place in cold water. Remove the shell and cut up, add to the sauce. Add a few drops of lemon juice carefully.

Bechamel Sauce.

Stock	½ pint.	Butter	2 ozs.
Milk	½ pint.	Flour	2 ozs.
Carrot, Onion, Celery, small piece		Peppercorns	10.
Bay leaf	1.		

Place the vegetables, seasoning, and bay leaf in a saucepan with the milk and stock, bring to the boil, and simmer 10 minutes. Melt the butter in a saucepan, stir in the flour and cook till granulated, but do not brown, strain in the milk and stock and whisk until quite smooth. Serve over boiled fowl, rabbit or veal.

Mutton (Boiled).

Boiling Water	1 pint.	Neck of Mutton	1 lb.
Onion, Carrot, Turnip	1.	Salt,	¼ teaspnful

Put the water on to boil. Take the yellow gristle and white cord from the joint. Wipe the meat with a damp cloth. Add salt to the water. When it boils, put in the meat and vegetables. Take off the scum. Simmer the meat for 1¼ hour, or until tender.

Prepare the Caper Sauce.

Butter	½ oz.	Capers	2 teaspoonsful.
Flour	½ oz.	Salt.	
Milk or Stock	¼ pint.	Pepper.	

Melt the butter in a saucepan. Stir in the flour, add the milk. Stir. Boil for 5 minutes. Cut the capers in halves, add them and a little vinegar to the sauce gradually. Season.

Place the mutton on a hot dish. Pour the sauce over.

Rabbit (Boiled).

| Rabbit | 1. | Boiling Water. |
| Bacon rolls | 6. | Carrot, turnip, onion 1. |

If necessary, paunch the rabbit. Cut off the first joint of the legs. Loosen the skin at the stomach, draw it up to the back, slip the hind legs out of the skin, skin the tail. Pull the skin towards the head till the fore legs are reached. Slip the fore legs out of the skin. Use a knife to skin the head, cut off the ears, take out the eyes. Draw away the heart, liver, lungs, and kidneys; clean them, and put them in the water. If there are many wounds in the rabbit, wash it. Wipe the inside of the rabbit with a damp cloth. Hang the head to soak in a basin of warm salt water. Cut across the sinews under the knees. Draw the hind legs forward, and the fore legs backward, till they overlap. Put the trussing needle through the legs where they overlap. (Leave an end of string). Run the needle through the body to the opposite side. Strike the point where the legs overlap. Pass the needle back again to the other side, a little above the fore knee-joints. Tie the ends of string. Turn the head round to the side of the body. On the opposite side to the head insert the trussing needle through the thick part of the shoulder. Pass it through the body and through the eyeholes, the neck, and back to the other side an inch higher than the starting point; tighten the string and tie the two ends. Skim the water in the saucepan. Put the rabbit in with the vegetables. Simmer gently for $\frac{3}{4}$ to 1 hour.

PREPARE THE ONION SAUCE.

Flour	1 oz.	Boiling Water	1 pint.
Milk	$\frac{1}{2}$ pint.	Butter	1 oz.
Onions	$\frac{1}{4}$ lb.	Salt.	
Cold Water	1 pint.	Pepper.	

Braid the flour with one tablespoonful of cold milk. Add the rest of the milk. Let it stand. Skin the onions, put them on in cold water, and bring them to a boil. Throw away the water. Pour on the boiling water. Boil $\frac{1}{2}$ hour, or till tender. Strain the water from the onions. Chop them. Rinse the saucepan. Put the flour and milk into it, stir, and boil well for 5 minutes. Add the butter and the onions. Season.

Remove the strings from the rabbit, place it on a hot dish. Pour the sauce over, and garnish with the cooked bacon rolls.

GRILLED MEAT.

Grilled Steak à la Maitre d'Hotel. No. 1.

Steak   1 lb. | Maître d'Hotel Butter ½ oz.
                     Potatoes 4.

Make the Maître d'Hotel butter as for kidneys on toast, and cut the potatoes into ribbons. Grease the bars of the gridiron, grill the steak for about 10 or 15 minutes, according to the thickness. It should be red in the centre when cooked. Serve on a hot dish, with the butter on the top, and the ribbon fried a golden brown placed round.

Grilled Steak. No. 2.

Onion	1.	Rump Steak	1 lb.
Dripping	1 oz.	Salt.	
Pepper.		Butter	¼ oz.

Have a clear fire, or make the grill of a gas stove red hot. Skin the onion, and slice it into rings. Heat the fat, fry the onion. If necessary, trim the meat. Heat the grill and grease it. Pepper the meat. Place it on the grid. Turn it when necessary. Put on a hot dish, sprinkle with salt, place the butter on top, and then the onions.

Kidneys on Toast.

Kidneys	2.	Cayenne Pepper, a few grains.
Butter	½ oz.	Lemon Juice	1 teaspoonful.
Parsley	1 teaspoonful chopped.	Toast	2 rounds.
		Potatoes	2.

Mix the butter, parsley, cayenne and lemon juice together with a wood spoon, form into a pat and put aside to cool until wanted for garnish.

Cut the potatoes into even sized matches, and fry them a light brown. Skin the kidneys, split them open, take out core, and run a skewer through to keep them open, put them on a gridiron, the cut side first to the fire, turn and grill for about seven minutes. They should be slightly underdone. Place them on the toast previously buttered, sprinkle pepper and salt over each kidney, and place a small pat of Maître d'Hotel butter on each. Serve the potatoes round.

RE-HEATING OF COOKED MATERIAL.

Croûtes of Fish.

Cooked Fish	3 or 4 ozs.	Cochineal.	
Parsley	1 sprig.	Cayenne.	
Tinned Tomato and Cornflour	1 tblspn.	Stale Bread	3 fingers.
		Milk	1 tablespoon.
Or Tomato Sauce	1 tblspn.	Frying fat.	

Heat the fat. Remove the bones and skin from the fish, break it up. Wash the parsley, dry and chop it. If tinned tomato is used rub it through a hair sieve and thicken with cornflour. Colour and season. Cut the fingers of bread 3 inches long, $1\frac{1}{2}$ inches wide, and $\frac{1}{4}$ inch thick. Dip in milk. Drain.

When the fat is hot enough fry them a *light* golden brown. Remove on to soft paper, then on to a hot dish. Make the tomato and fish very hot in a saucepan. Season. Lift out with a spoon on to the fried bread. Sprinkle chopped parsley over.

N.B.—If there are no remains of tomato in the larder use anchovy sauce or white sauce with anchovy essence added. If the fish is herring use mustard sauce.

Croûtes of Meat.

Stale Bread	3 squares.	Sauce (brown or white)	1 tspn.
Butter	$1\frac{1}{2}$ oz.	Condiment Sauce	1 tspn.
Cooked Meat	3 or 4 oz.	Coloured Bread Crumbs.	

Cut 3 squares of bread 2 inches long, 2 inches wide, and $\frac{1}{4}$ inch thick. Melt the butter in a small frying pan, remove the scum, let it stand. Take away the skin and gristle from the meat, mince it finely. Pour the melted butter off the sediment, rub out the pan, return the butter. Fry the bread a *light* golden brown. Drain on soft paper, and place on hot dish. Make the meat and sauce very hot in the frying pan; lift the mixture on to the bread. Sprinkle with coloured crumbs (brown or red).

N.B.—Condiment Sauce, viz., Worcester, Harvey, Ketchup, Curry.

Croquettes (Meat).

Frying Fat		Cooked Meat	4 to 6 ozs.
Small Onion	¼.	Ketchup	1 teaspn.
Fat	¼ oz.	Salt	¼ saltspn.
Flour	¼ oz.	Pepper	a dust.
Stock	¾ gill.	Stale Crumb of Bread	2 ozs.
Parsley	4 sprigs.	Egg	1.

Put the frying fat to heat slowly. Skin the onion and chop it. Heat ¼ oz. fat in a saucepan, brown the onion in it; add flour, and brown. Stir in the stock, and boil; remove from the fire. Wash the parsley, dry it, put by three sprigs, chop the fourth. Mince the meat finely; remove gristle, fat, and skin. Stir the parsley, meat and ketchup into the gravy; season. Prepare the breadcrumbs, beat the egg on a plate, place a double fold of soft paper on a baking sheet. Divide the croquette mixture into six equal portions. Flour the hands lightly. Form the mixture into balls; pass them one by one through the egg and crumbs; shake off loose crumbs; roll lightly in the hands. Place the balls in the frying fat; fry them a golden brown; drain on paper. Fry the parsley; drain. Dish the croquettes on paper, and garnish with parsley.

Rissoles.

Mixture as above.		Short Crust Pastry	3 ozs.
Egg	1	Stale Bread Crumbs	2 ozs.

Divide the mixture into six equal portions; roll out the pastry very thinly, and cut out with round cutter. Place one portion of the mixture in each round, wet the edges, and join.

Carefully egg and breadcrumb each rissole, and fry in deep fat until golden brown. Drain on paper, dish on a folded d'Oyley, and garnish with fried parsley.

Curry.

Curry Paste	½ teaspoonful.	Small Onion	1 oz.
Curry Powder	2 tspns.	Cooked Meat	4 to 6 ozs.
Flour	1 teaspoonful.	Stock or Milk	½ pint.
Apple	½ teaspoonful.	Salt	½ saltspn.
Fat	½ oz.	Lemon Juice.	

Make the fat hot in the pan. Skin the onion, cut it up, cook it in the fat. Add curry powder, flour, and paste, stock or milk, apple and lemon. Stir and boil for 15 minutes. Cool this gravy. Cut the meat in small squares. Put gravy and meat into a saucepan. Simmer 30 minutes. Season.

Prepare the Boiled Rice.

Boiling Water	3 quarts.	Patna Rice	4 to 6 ozs.
Salt	1 tspn.	Cold Water	1 pint.

When the water boils fast, add the salt. Sprinkle in the rice. Do not allow the water to stop boiling. Boil fast for 10 to 15 minutes. When the rice grains are soft, add cold water. Strain *at once*. Leave the rice in the hot saucepan on the hob to dry with the lid tilted. Shake the rice occasionally, or raise it with a fork. Form it into a wall on a hot dish. Place the curry in the centre, or serve the rice on separate dish.

Meat or Fish Scallops.

Cooked Meat or Fish	3 or 4 oz.	Pepper	A pinch.
Butter	¾ oz.	Salt	¼ saltspoon.
Brown Bread Crumbs	1 tblspn.	Lemon Juice.	
	Stock or Milk, 3 teaspoonsful.		

Butter three shells or patty pans (3 inch), coat with breadcrumbs. Remove bones and skin from the fish and break it up, or mince the meat finely. Add salt, pepper, lemon juice, and mix all well together. Fill the shells or patty pans, pour in stock or milk. Sprinkle on crumbs. Place small pieces of butter over the surface. Bake in a moderate oven for 10 minutes. Serve in the pans or shells.

Fricassee of Chicken or Veal.

Remains of Cooked Chicken or Veal.

Milk	½ pt.	Flour	1½ oz.
Chicken or veal stock flavoured with vegetables	¼ pt.	Bacon	6 roils.
		Blades Mace	2.
		Peppercorns	6.
Butter	1½ oz.	Croûtes (fried bread)	6.

Cut the meat into neat pieces for serving, and remove any skin. Make a sauce with the butter, flour, milk, stock, mace, and peppercorns. Boil well, and season with salt to taste. Put in the meat and simmer very gently for about ½ hour, or until the meat is thoroughly heated through. Cook the bacon and fry the croûtes. Dish up the fowl or veal on a hot dish, Strain the sauce over and garnish with the bacon and croûtes, and if liked some pieces of vegetables cut in fancy shapes. Sometimes a teaspoonful of anchovy essence is an improvement to this dish.

Note.—The yokes of 2 eggs can be added to the sauce if a richer stew is wanted. They should be added just before serving.

Kromeskies.

For batter:
- Flour — 2 ozs.
- Salad Oil — ½ tblspn.
- Tepid Water — ½ gill.
- White of Egg — 1.
- Salt.
- Pepper.

- Cooked Fish or Meat — 2 ozs.
- Fat Bacon — 2 slices.
- Cold Sauce — 1 tspn.
- Lemon Juice — 2 drops.
- Cayenne.
- Salt.

Frying Fat.

Put flour in basin; make a hole in the centre, put the oil in this. Add the water. Stir the flour in gradually. Beat it well. Leave to stand. Put the fat on to heat. Break up the fish, pick out the bones; add sauce, lemon juice, cayenne, and salt. Mix well. Cut thin slices of bacon. Roll up the mixture in these. Break the egg, put the white on to a plate. Whip it up stiffly. Stir it into the batter very lightly. Dip in the rolls. Drop them into the fat. Drain on soft paper.

BREAKFAST DISHES AND SAVOURIES.

Fresh Herrings.

- Onion — 1.
- Peppercorns — 6.
- Vinegar — ¼ pint.
- Fresh Herrings — 2.
- Flour — ¼ oz.
- Mustard — ½ teaspn.

Have a clear fire or make the grill of a gas stove red hot. Skin the onion. Simmer it with the peppercorns in vinegar for quarter of an hour. Clean the fish, trim, dry, and notch them across with a knife. Flour and broil them. Melt the butter, mix in the flour and mustard. Strain in the vinegar. Stir and boil. Place the herrings on a dish and pour sauce over.

Kedgeree.

- Egg — 1.
- Dried Haddock — ½ lb.
- Boiling Water — 2 quarts.
- Salt.
- Lemon Juice — few drops.
- Patna Rice — 4 ozs.
- Parsley.
- Butter — 1½ ozs.

Pepper.

Put the water on to boil for the egg. Cook the haddock. Put the egg in boiling water and boil for 13 minutes. Crack the shell and place in cold water. Boil water for rice. Add salt and lemon juice. When the water boils sprinkle the rice in. Do not allow the water to stop boiling. Boil fast for about 15 minutes. Shell the egg and cut it into large dice. Wash the parsley, dry, and chop it. When the rice grains are soft add cold water and drain *at once*. Leave the rice in the hot saucepan on the hob to dry with the lid tilted. Shake it occasionally, or raise with a fork. Take the fish from the pan, break it into flakes, remove bones and skin. Put the butter, fish, and white of egg in the saucepan with the rice: season. Make it very hot. Turn it on to the dish in a pile.

Garnish with powdered egg and parsley.

Scotch Eggs.

| Eggs | 3. | Sausages | 1. |
| Frying Fat. | | Breadcrumbs | ¼ lb. |

Tomato Sauce, ¼ pint.

Put two eggs into boiling water and boil for 13 minutes. Put the fat on to heat. Make the tomato sauce. Crack the eggs and put them in cold water. Remove the shell, dry and flour them. Cut off one tip of the sausage; press the knife on the other. Squeeze out the meat. Coat the eggs with this. Break the raw egg on a plate, beat it; put crumbs on paper. Roll the coated eggs in the raw egg, then in the crumbs. Shake off loose crumbs. Press on those that adhere. Fry a golden brown. Drain on soft paper. Cut the eggs in halves. Put the cut side upwards and pour sauce round. The eggs look better if served on croûtes of fried bread.

Tomato Sauce.

Onion	1.	Sprig Thyme.	
Lean Ham	½ oz.	Peppercorns	4.
Butter	¼ oz.	Vinegar.	1 tablespn.
Bay Leaf	1.	Tinned Tomatoes	½ lb.

Cornflour, ½ oz.

Skin the onion. Cut up the ham and the onion. Melt the butter, put in the ham, onion, bay leaf, thyme, peppercorns, fry for a few minutes, and add vinegar and tomato. Simmer 15 minutes. Rub the tomato through a hair sieve. Return to saucepan and re-heat. Mix the cornflour with a little cold water, add to sauce, and boil to thicken.

Spiced Mackerel.

Peppercorns	8.	Water	1 pint.
Vinegar	½ pint.	Salt	1 teaspoonful.
Mackerel	1.	Cayenne.	
	Fennel.		

Boil the peppercorns in the vinegar for 30 minutes, till it is reduced to half the quantity. Let it get cold. Trim and clean the fish. Put it into a saucepan of cold water, add salt, bring to the boil slowly. Take out the fish and put into a pie-dish. Mix quarter pint of the liquor with the vinegar; add cayenne and salt; pour over fish. Souce for 12 hours closely covered. Remove from vinegar before sending it to table. Garnish with fennel.

Sovoury Omelet.

Parsley 1 teaspn. chopped.	Seasoning.	
Eggs 2.	Onion	a small piece.
Butter	¾ oz	

Melt the butter in a small frying pan. Beat the eggs until yolks and whites are thoroughly mixed, add chopped parsley and seasoning. Fry the onion for a few minutes, remove it and pour in the eggs, stir quickly with a fork until nearly set, roll up towards the outside of the pan. Brown slightly, and turn into a hot dish.

Cheese omelet may be made in the same way using ¾ oz. of grated cheese instead of the parsley and onion.

Anchovy Toast.

Anchovy Fillets	3.	Cayenne	A few grains.
Butter	1 oz.	Croûtes of Bread	6
Egg	1.	Parsley	1 teaspoonful (chopped).

Boil the egg hard. Fry the croûtes. Pound the anchovies with the butter and yolk and half the white of egg, add the seasoning; rub this mixture through a wire sieve. Place in a forcing bag, and cover each croûte with some of the mixture. Garnish with chopped white of egg and parsley.

Cheese Pudding.

Butter	½ oz.	Cheese	1 oz., grated.
Milk	1 gill.	Egg	1 large.
Bread Crumbs	2 ozs.	Mustard	½ saltspoonful.
	Seasoning.		

Melt the butter in the milk. Mix the bread crumbs, cheese, salt, mustard; add to the milk. Beat the yolk and add it to the mixture. Whip the white to a stiff froth, lightly stir into the mixture. Bake in a greased pie dish 15 minutes.

Cheese Fondue.

Butter	½ oz.	Eggs	1 yolk 2 whites.
Flour	¼ oz.	Parmesan Cheese	
Milk	½ gill.		1½ oz. grated.
Peppercorns ½ teaspoonful.		Cayenne	a few grains.

Melt the butter in a saucepan, and fry the peppercorns for a few minutes, then remove them. Add the flour, seasoning, and milk. Stir over the fire till the mixture thickens. Remove from the fire. Beat in 1 yolk of egg and add the cheese. Whisk the whites to a stiff froth and stir in very lightly. Pour into greased ramequin cases, and bake in a quick oven about 10 minutes. Sprinkle a little cheese over the top, and serve at once. If a single fondue case is used, double the above quantity of mixture will be required.

Macaroni Cheese.

Water	1 qt.	Butter	½ oz.
Salt	1 teaspoonful.	Flour	¼ oz.
Macaroni	1 oz.	Milk	½ pt.
Dry Cheese	1½ ozs.	Mixed Mustard.	
Slice of Bread.		Cayenne.	

Put the water on to boil. Break the macaroni in small pieces. When the water boils, add the salt and macaroni. Boil for 20 minutes, or till tender. Grate the cheese. Drain the water off the macaroni and put it on a plate. Dissolve half the butter in the saucepan, stir in the flour, add the milk gradually, stir well, and let it boil. Add more milk if too thick. Add mustard, cayenne, macaroni, and half the cheese.

Put the mixture in a dish, sprinkle the rest of the cheese over, place small pieces of butter on top; brown.

Potted Meat.

Lean Beef	1 lb.	Butter	3 oz.
Allspice	2.	Blade of Mace	1.
Clove	1.	Anchovies	2.
Peppercorns	2.	Salt.	
Bayleaf	1.	Pepper.	

Butter the inside of a stone jar, put the meat and anchovies into it, shredding the meat finely, add the spices tied in muslin. Cover with a greased paper and cook gently for two hours in a moderate oven. Remove the spices, pound the beef and anchovies in a mortar, rub through a wire sieve, add the butter melted. Put into pots and cover with clarified butter, or lard.

Potted Shrimps.

| Picked Shrimps | ¼ pint. | Blades Mace | 2. |
| Butter | 2 ozs. | | |

Simmer the butter and mace until the butter is well flavoured, but do not brown it. Take out the mace and put in the shrimps. Stir them into the butter, take off the fire and pour into a pot. When quite cold cover over with clarified butter, or lard.

Curried Eggs.

Eggs (Hard Boiled)	2.	Curry Powder	1 teaspoonful.
Rice (Boiled)	¼ lb.	Flour	1 teaspoonful.
Butter	¾ oz.	Stock	¼ pint.
1 small piece Onion and Apple.		Salt.	
	Lemon Juice.		

Chop the onion and apple and fry in the butter for 5 or 6 minutes without browning, stir in the curry powder and flour. Mix well and fry for a few minutes, add the stock and salt. Simmer for 10 or 15 minutes. Add lemon juice. Cut up the eggs into 4 pieces and put them into the curry to re-heat. Place the rice in a border on a hot dish and pour the curry into the centre.

SAUCE.

Horseradish Sauce.

| Mustard | ½ teaspoonful. | White Vinegar | 1 teaspoonful. |
| Horseradish | 1 stick. | Cream, thick | 2 tablespnfls. |

Grate the horseradish quite finely, add to it some salt and the mustard and vinegar; mix well together and stir in the cream. Leave in a cold place till wanted. Serve in sauceboat with roast beef.

VEGETABLES AND SALADS.

Mashed Potato.

| Boiled Potato | 6 ozs. | Milk | 1 tablespoonful. |
| Butter | ¼ oz. | Seasoning. | |

If the potatoes are cold, warm them. Dissolve the butter in the milk. Rub the potato through a sieve; add milk, butter, and seasoning. Work them smooth with a wooden spoon.

Potato Chips.

Potatoes ¼ lb. | Fat for frying.

Put the pan of fat on to heat. Scrub the potatoes, wash and pare them, cut them in thin slices into cold water. Drain and thoroughly dry them. Fry in deep fat for about 3 minutes; take them out; let the fat get smoking hot; put the potatoes in again. Fry a light brown. Drain on soft paper, and sprinkle with salt.

Potato Croquettes.

Parsley	½ teaspoonful.	Egg	1.
Potatoes	½ lb.	Seasoning.	
Butter	¼ oz.	Stale Crumb of Bread	1½ oz.
Milk	1 teaspoonful.	Frying Fat.	

Prepare the potatoes and boil them in the usual way; let them be dry. Put the fat on to heat. Wash the parsley, dry and chop it, keep the stalks. Rub the potatoes through a sieve, add the parsley; dissolve the butter in the milk. Separate the white and yolk, put a little of the yolk with the potato. Add the milk, butter, and seasoning; mix all together thoroughly. Form the mixture into shape; beat up the remainder of the egg on a plate; prepare the bread crumbs. Pass the croquettes through the egg and crumbs, one by one; place in a frying basket. When the fat is hot enough plunge in the basket, and fry the croquettes a light golden brown. Put in stalks of parsley.

Salad.

Lettuce, 1.

Pick the leaves of the lettuce apart, but leave the heart whole. Wash thoroughly and drain. Dry. Shake in a basket or cloth.

Salad Dressing.

Hard-boiled Yolk	1.	Pepper	a pinch.
Made Mustard	½ teaspn.	Oil	1 tablespoonful.
Sugar	a pinch.	Vinegar	½ tablespoonful.
Salt	a pinch.		

Work the yolk in a basin, put in the mustard, salt, sugar, and pepper. Add the oil gradually, stir all the time with a wooden spoon. Do not hurry the mixing. Add the vinegar and mix in the lettuce. Put the salad into a bowl. Arrange lettuce on top and the heart in the centre. Use a garnish, such as watercress, cucumber, tomato, endive, mustard and cress, beetroot, radish, and hard-boiled egg.

Mayonnaise Sauce.

Egg raw	1 yolk.	Vinegar	1 teaspn.
Salad Oil	½ gill.	Tarragon Vinegar	1 teaspn.

Mustard, ¼ teaspoonful.

Place the yolk of an egg in a basin, add the salt, pepper, and mustard, pour in the salad oil one drop at a time, whisking quickly all the time. At the last stir in the vinegar.

This sauce should be quite smooth and thick.

Boiled Artichokes.

Artichokes	1 lb.	Water	2 qrts., boiling.
Salt	2 teaspn.	Vinegar	1 teaspoonful

Wash, scrub, and peel the artichokes thinly. Place in cold water with a little vinegar. Cook in boiling water about half hour or until quite tender, drain and serve with white sauce.

Stuffed Tomatoes.

Tomatoes	2.	Brown Sauce	1 dessertspn.
Ham	½ oz. chopped.	Seasoning—Nutmeg.	
Bread Crumbs	½ oz.	Brown Crumbs and	
Onion	¼ teaspoonful.	grated Cheese	1 dessertspn.
Parsley	½ teaspoonful.	Butter	½ oz.
Croûtes of Bread 2.			

Fry the croûtes of bread a golden brown. Remove the seeds from each tomato, and season each with pepper and salt. Melt butter, fry ham and other chopped ingredients, add brown sauce, nutmeg, seasoning. Fill each tomato with this mixture, and spread the remainder on each croûte. Place the tomatoes on the croûtes, and cook for 10 minutes in a moderate oven. Sprinkle each with the cheese and brown crumbs, serve on a folded paper. Garnish with parsley.

Cauliflower au Gratin.

Cauliflower	1	Flour	$\frac{1}{2}$ oz
Grated Parmesan Cheese	$1\frac{1}{2}$ oz.	Water	$\frac{1}{4}$ pint.
Butter	$\frac{1}{2}$ oz.	Cayenne Pepper and Salt.	

Take a moderate-sized cauliflower, trim and clean it, and put to soak in salt and water for half-an-hour.

Cook it quickly in plenty of boiling water and salt, keeping the flower under the water. It will take 30 to 50 minutes to cook. Drain and press the flower well together, to make a smooth surface. Pour the sauce over the cauliflower (it should be quite thick and not run off the flower), sprinkle the remainder of the cheese over, and brown in a very quick oven or in front of the fire. Serve very hot.

SAUCE.

Melt the butter, add the flour, cook, and add the water, boil a few minutes, cool, and add half the cheese and the seasoning.

NOTE.—The cauliflower may be divided up into small portions after it is cooked and put into small greased scallop shells, sauced over and finished in the same way as above.

French Beans.

The beans should be perfectly fresh. Peel off the thin string on each side and cut the beans into thin slices crosswise. Place them in cold water for at least $\frac{1}{4}$ hour. Have ready a saucepan with plenty of boiling water, well salted. Put in the beans and boil quickly without the lid until they are tender, about 25 to 40 minutes. Drain off the water and add a small piece of butter to the beans. Serve in hot vegetable dish.

Celery and Sea Kale.

Celery	1 head.	Water	$\frac{1}{4}$ pint.
Butter	$\frac{1}{2}$ oz.	Pepper and Salt.	
Flour	$\frac{1}{2}$ oz.	1 Slice of Toast cut in four.	

Well wash and scrub the celery and cut into convenient sized pieces.

Boil in plenty of fast-boiling water, well salted, until tender, 30 to 40 minutes. Drain and serve in a vegetable dish on toast with melted butter sauce over.

Sauce.

Melt the butter, add the flour and cook for a few minutes, pour in the water, season, and stir until the sauce is well cooked. Pour over the celery.

NOTE.—The sea kale is cooked and served in the same manner, but should be tied in bundles.

Carrot Mould.

Wash and scrape 3 large carrots, boil them for 2 hours, drain and rub through a sieve. Melt 1 oz. butter and beat it well into the carrots; beat up an egg and add to the mixture, season with pepper and salt, and pour into a greased mould, pressing it well down. Bake for 10 minutes in a hot oven; turn into a hot dish and sprinkle some chopped parsley on the top, and serve.

PUDDINGS.

Castle Pudding.

Egg	1.	Butter	weight of egg.
Sugar	weight of egg.	Lemon Rind	a little.
Flour	weight of egg.	Baking Powder	$\frac{1}{4}$ teaspoonful.

Ascertain the weight of the egg, to be able to obtain the other ingredients. Butter 4 large darioles. Cream sugar, and butter together. Beat the egg; add flour and egg alternately, stir lightly. Grate the lemon rind, and stir it in to the mixture with the baking powder. Half-fill the darioles. Bake $\frac{1}{2}$ hour in a moderate oven.

Prepare the Jam Sauce.

Water	$\frac{1}{4}$ pint.	Jam	2 tblspn.
Loaf Sugar	2 oz.	Lemon Juice	$\frac{1}{2}$ tblspn.
	Carmine.		

Melt the sugar in the water. Stir in the jam. Boil 10 minutes. Add lemon juice and colouring. Place the puddings on a dish. Pour the sauce round.

French Rice Pudding.

Rice	1½ oz.	Raisins	1½ oz.
Milk	½ pint.	Candied Peel	1½ oz.
Suet	1½ oz.	Sugar	1½ oz.
Egg	1.	Fat to grease basin and paper.	

Put a saucepan of water on to boil. Grease basin and paper. Wash the rice, stew it in the milk till the milk is absorbed. Prepare the suet, raisins, and peel. Stir these, the egg and sugar into the rice. Put the mixture into the basin, cover it and steam 1½ to 2 hours. Turn out and pour a sweet sauce round.

Snowdon Pudding.

Raisins	1½ oz.	Salt	a pinch.
Stale Crumb of Bread	2 oz.	Lemon Rind	½ oz.
Suet	1½ oz.	Egg	1.
Ground Rice	¾ oz.	Marmalade	1½ oz.
Castor Sugar	1½ oz.	Milk ?	¼ gill.
Baking Powder	½ teasp.		

Fat to grease basin and paper.

Put the water on to boil. Grease the basin and paper. Slit the raisins open, do not divide the two halves. Press the cut side against greased basin. Prepare the bread crumbs and suet, mix into these the ground rice, sugar, salt, and lemon rind. Beat the egg, mix it with the marmalade, stir these into the dry ingredients. If necessary, use some milk. Pour into the ornamented basin. Cover with paper and steam 2 to 3 hours.

PREPARE THE WHITE SAUCE.

Butter	¼ oz.	Milk and Water	¼ pint.
Flour	¼ oz.	Castor Sugar	¼ oz.

Vanilla Essence, ½ teaspoonful.

Melt the butter. Stir in the flour. Add the milk and water. Stir and boil. Sweeten and flavour.

Place the pudding on a hot dish and pour the sauce round.

Syrup Pudding.

Fat to grease basin.		Flour	¼ lb.
Stale Crumb of Bread	1½ oz.	Salt	a pinch.
Lemon Rind	a strip.	Water.	
Suet	2 oz.	Golden Syrup	2 tblspns.

Put water on to boil. Grease the basin. Prepare the bread crumbs, lemon rind, and suet. Mix the flour and salt. Add the suet and water. Form a stiff paste. Divide the paste into one large and four small pieces. Flour board and pin. Roll out the large piece and line the basin; cover the bottom with syrup, bread crumbs, and lemon rind. Roll the four small pieces of paste into rounds the size of the basin. Repeat alternate layers of paste and the mixture until the basin is quite full. Wet the edge of the paste, put on the lid, seal the edges. Tie a cloth over, plunge into boiling water, and boil 2 hours.

Apple Amber.

Apples	$\frac{3}{4}$ lb.	Salt.	
Butter	$1\frac{1}{2}$ oz.	Butter	$\frac{1}{2}$ oz.
Moist Sugar	2 ozs.	Lard	1 oz.
Lemon Rind.		Water.	
Flour	2 ozs.	Lemon Juice.	

Eggs 2.

Pare the apples, core and slice them. Put them in a pan with the butter, sugar, and lemon rind. Stew slowly till soft. Sieve the salt and flour. Cut the butter and lard into small pieces mix these into the flour. Keep them in lumps. Add lemon juice and water and form the paste. Flour board and pin. Roll out the paste with a short forward push till it becomes long, thin and narrow. Fold in three, keep the edges even, press them with the pin, turn the smooth edge to the right hand, roll out as before, and fold again. Put aside to get cool. Rub the fruit through a hair sieve. Separate the whites and yolks of the eggs. Beat the yolks and mix them with the pure apple. Repeat the rolling and folding of the pastry three times. Brush a little white of egg on the edge of the dish; line the edge and sides, cut stars of pastry and decorate the edge. Pour the mixture into the dish. Bake in a quick oven for 15 minutes. Whip the whites up stiffly. Pile them on to the dish. Dredge with castor-sugar. Brown lightly in a slow oven.

Caramel Custards.

Loaf Sugar	2 ozs.	White of Egg	1.
Water	2 tblspns.	Castor Sugar	$\frac{1}{2}$ oz.
Milk	$\frac{1}{4}$ pint.	Vanilla	
Yolks	2.		

Put four large darioles on a baking sheet. Melt the sugar and water, and let it brown on the stove. Put the milk on to heat. Beat up the eggs. Run the caramel round to coat the sides of the darioles. Stand. Stir the sugar and vanilla into the milk. Pour these on to the egg, mix well. Fill the dariole moulds. Butter some paper and cover them. Place in a saucepan of boiling water for about 30 minutes about 2 inches deep. The water should not boil after the pudding is in, only simmer gently. Loosen the edges and turn out.

French Pancakes.

Milk	¼ pint.	Egg	1.
Butter	1 oz.	Flour	1 oz.
Sugar	1 oz.	Jam.	

Put the milk on to boil, and grease 2 saucers. Cream butter and sugar together. Beat the egg. Stir the flour and egg in gradually. Add the milk. Beat well. Let it stand one hour or longer. Stir the batter, pour it into the saucers. Raise in a quick oven. Bake in moderate oven 15 minutes. Loosen carefully with a knife. Turn out, spread with jam, fold over, sugar, and serve hot.

Semolina Soufflée.

| Milk | ½ pint. | Loaf Sugar | 1 oz. |
| Semolina | 1½ oz. | Egg | 2 whites 1 yolk. |

Fat to grease soufflée tin and paper.

Put the saucepan of water on to boil. Grease the soufflée tin and paper. Heat the milk, sprinkle in the semolina. Stir, and boil till it thickens and the semolina becomes transparent; add the sugar. Separate the yolk and white of egg. When the semolina is cool, beat in the yolk. Whip the white up stiffly. Mix it in lightly. Pour into the greased tin. Cover with paper. When the water boils, place the soufflée in a steamer, or in a saucepan with the water three-parts up the tin. Steam *very gently* half to three-quarters of an hour.

PREPARE THE JAM SAUCE.

| Water | ¼ pint. | Raspberry Jam | 2 tblspn. |
| Loaf Sugar | 2 ozs. | Lemon Juice | few drops. |

Cochineal, few drops.

Put the water, sugar, and jam into a saucepan, boil uncovered until it becomes a thick syrup. Add lemon juice and cochineal. Take the soufflée from the pan and stand 2 or 3 minutes. Loosen the top with fingers. Turn out. Strain the sauce round the soufflée.

Bread and Butter Pudding.

Loaf Sugar	1 oz.	Butter	1 oz.
Milk	½ pint.	Stale Bread	1 round of loaf.
Currants or Sultanas	1 oz.	Egg	1.

Put the sugar in the milk to melt. Wash the currants, dry, pick, and test them. If Sultanas are used, flour them and remove stalks. Butter the pie dish and the bread. Cut this into convenient sized pieces. Lay them in the dish. Scatter the fruit between. Beat the egg. Add it to the milk, stir. Pour this custard over the bread. Let all stand to soak half-an-hour. Bake in moderate oven half-an-hour.

Apple Charlotte.

Apples	1 lb.	Water	1 gill.
Lemon	½ rind and juice.	Bread	Stale slice.
Sugar	¼ lb.	Butter	4 ozs.

1 plain round tin mould.

Slice the apples and put them into a stewpan with the sugar, water, lemon rind and juice; when quite soft rub through a sieve. Cut the bread into rounds, two large to fit the bottom and top of the mould, and the remainder into small rounds. Line the mould with the bread passed through the clarified butter. Fill the mould with the apple, and place a large round of bread on the top, cover with a saucer and weight; bake for 1 hour. Turn out and serve with the remainder of the apple.

Queen's Pudding.

Milk	½ pint.	Egg	1.
Bread Crumbs	2 ozs.	Lemon	½ rind grated.
Butter	1 oz	Sugar	1 oz.

Jam 2 tablespoonfuls.

Prepare the pie dish as for apple amber. Melt the butter in the milk, pour on to the breadcrumbs, and add yolk of egg; bake in prepared pie dish in a moderately quick oven until set, about 20 minutes; spread jam on the top, finish with whipped white of egg and bake in cool oven till crisp.

Chocolate Pudding.

Chocolate	2 oz.	Butter	1½ oz
Milk	1 gill.	Sugar	1½ oz.
Bread Crumbs (fresh)	3 oz.	Eggs	1½

Vanilla 1 teaspoonful.

Shred the chocolate and dissolve it in the milk. Cream the butter and sugar together, and add the yolk of egg; add the bread crumbs and chocolate alternately. Stir in lightly the white of egg, beaten to a stiff froth; add the vanilla, turn into a well-greased mould, and steam 1½ hours. Serve with custard sauce round.

CUSTARD SAUCE.

Egg	1	Vanilla	1 teaspoonful.
Milk	1 gill.	Sugar	1 teaspoonful.

Break the egg into a saucepan, add the sugar, milk, and vanilla; whisk over the fire till it thickens, taking care that it does not curdle.

Lemon Pudding, No. 1.

Butter	3 oz.	Rind of Lemons	2.
Sugar	3 oz.	Eggs	2.
Flour	4 oz.	Baking Powder	¼ teaspoon.

Cream, butter and sugar together; beat the eggs well. Grate the lemon rind into the flour, and add to the creamed mixture alternately with the egg. Add the baking powder with the last of the flour. If the mixture is too stiff, add a little lemon juice. Put into a well greased mould, and steam for 1¼ hours. Serve with lemon sauce.

Lemon Pudding, No. 2.

Bread Crumbs	4 oz.	Sugar	4 oz.
Suet	4 oz.	Lemons	2.
Flour	3 oz.	Eggs	2.

Milk 1 gill.

Chop the suet finely with the bread crumbs and add to the other dry ingredients and grated lemon rind and juice. Mix the milk with the eggs, beat well together, and pour into dry ingredients; when well mixed place in a greased basin, cover with paper and steam 5 hours. Serve with sweet melted butter or lemon sauce.

Marmalade Pudding.

Bread Crumbs	4 oz.	Lemon	1.
Suet	2 oz.	Egg	1.
Canpied Peel	2 oz.	Marmalade	3 tablesps.
Baking Powder	½ teasp.	Milk	1 gill.

Chop the suet finely with the bread crumbs, shred the candied peel and grate the lemon rind. Place all the dry ingredients in a basin, and mix with the marmalade, egg and milk. Pour in a greased basin, steam 3 to 5 hours. Serve with marmalade sauce.

Marmalade Sauce.

Cornflour	$\frac{1}{2}$ oz.	Sugar	1 tablespoonful.
Marmalade	1 tablespoonful.	Water, boiling,	$\frac{1}{2}$ pint.
Lemon rind and juice.			

Mix cornflour with lemon juice, infuse the lemon rind in the water. Strain. Bring to boil and pour into the cornflour. Return to saucepan, add sugar and marmalade, reduce and pour round pudding.

Sweet Omelet.

Eggs	3.	Vanilla	1 teaspoonful.
Sugar	$1\frac{1}{2}$ oz.	Jam	2 dessert spoons.

Place the yolks in a small basin with the sugar, and whisk until quite stiff. Add the vanilla. Add pinch of salt to the whites, and whisk very stiffly. Stir lightly into the thickened yolks, and pour it into a pan greased with clarified butter. Bake in a quick oven 10 or 15 minutes. Heat the jam. When cooked turn the omelet on to a paper sprinkled with sugar, spread jam over, half fold the omelet over. Serve at once on a folded paper.

Treacle Sponge.

Flour	$\frac{1}{2}$ lb.	Ground Ginger	$\frac{3}{4}$ oz.
Suet	$\frac{1}{4}$ lb.	Treacle	1 gill.
Carbonate of Soda	$\frac{1}{2}$ teaspn.	Milk	$\frac{1}{4}$ pint.
Salt.		Egg	1.

Chop the suet as finely as possible, and put it into a basin with the flour, carbonate of soda, and ginger. Beat up the egg, mix the treacle and milk with it, and stir this into the mixture in the basin; add more milk if required to make the pudding moist. Grease a basin thoroughly, put the pudding mixture into it, cover with a greased paper. Have enough boiling water to come halfway up the basin in a saucepan, and steam for two hours, turn out, and serve with warmed treacle poured round.

COLD SWEETS.

Apple Jelly.

Apples	1 lb.	Lemon Rind.	
Loaf Sugar	2 ozs.	Lemon Juice	1 tspn.
Water	½ pint.	Gelatine (sheet)	¼ oz.
	Cochineal.		

Pare and core the apples. Cut them up. Melt the sugar in ¼ pint of water, put in the apples, lemon rind, and juice. Soften the fruit slowly. Melt the gelatine in ¼ pint of water. Rub the apples through a hair sieve. Stir in the gelatine. Fill the mould with cold water. Turn out the water. Pour in half the apple. Colour the remainder. Add when the first half is partly set. When cold turn out.

Lemon Jelly.

Cold Water	¾ pt.	Cloves	2.
Gelatine (sheet)	1 oz.	Lemons	2.
Loaf Sugar	3 ozs.	Juice and Water	¼ pint.
Cinnamon	½ in.	Egg (white & shell)	1.

Put the cloth through which the jelly is to be strained into a pan. Cover it with cold water. Bring to the boil. Rinse and put on stand.

Cut off the rinds of lemon thinly, and in small pieces; squeeze out the juice. Wash the egg; separate the white from the yolk; crush up the shell. Rinse the pan out with cold water; do not dry it. Beat the white of egg. Put all the ingredients in the pan. Whisk them over the fire till a thick froth rises all over the surface. Take out the whisk. Bring to the boil. When the scum cracks use less heat. Simmer five minutes. Stand in a warm place ten minutes.

Get two good sized basins; place one under the cloth. Pour boiling water through the cloth. Empty the basin and put it back. Pour the jelly on to the cloth. Change the basin. Return the first runnings to the cloth. If the jelly is not clear repeat this. Fill a mould with cold water. When the jelly is cool, turn the water from the mould, and pour in the jelly. When the jelly is set, dip the mould into sufficient warm water to cover it. Wipe the top with a cloth. Shake the mould; reverse it with one hand underneath; let the jelly slip gently till it touches the hand. Place it on the dish, and raise the mould carefully.

Lemon Sponge.

Lemons	2.	Loaf Sugar	2 oz.
Water	½ pint.	White of Egg	1.
Gelatine (sheet)	¼ oz.	Cochineal.	

Pare the lemon thinly. Put it in the water with the gelatine and sugar. Place over the fire. Put the white of egg in a basin. Squeeze and strain the lemon juice on to the egg. When the gelatine is thoroughly dissolved strain it on to the white of egg. Whisk till very stiff. Place two-thirds of the sponge roughly in a glass dish. Colour the remainder and pile on top.

Swiss Cream.

Castor Sugar	½ oz.	Jam	2 tablespoonfuls.
Egg	1	Almonds	4.
Milk (hot)	¼ pint.	Milk	2 tablespoonfuls.
Stale Sponge Cakes	2.	Essence of Almonds, few drops.	

Beat sugar and egg together. Add the milk. Put all in a jam-pot or jug. Stand in a saucepan of hot water. Boil the water and stir continually till the custard coats the spoon. Take out the jam-pot and stir the custard for five minutes. Flavour with the essence. Slit each cake in three. Spread jam on each piece. Re-shape the cakes. Place them in a glass dish. Prick holes, and soak with milk. Pour boiling water over the almonds; soak for 1 or 2 minutes; rub off the skin. Throw them into cold water. Cut each almond into six. Stick the pieces into the cake. Let it soak 1 hour. Pour the custard over.

Prune Mould.

Prunes	½ lb.	Lemon	½ rind & juice.
Water	1 pint.	Cochineal	¼ teaspoonful.
Gelatine dissolved	½ oz.	Castor sugar	1½ ozs.

Soak the prunes overnight. Boil the prunes and lemon rind in the water until quite soft. Make up water to 1 pint again. Remove the stones, crack the kernels, and add them with the lemon juice, rind, sugar, and gelatine. Boil all for 10 minutes, colour and pour into a mould, when set turn out.

Malvern Pudding.

Water	6 to 8 tblspns.	Fruit	½ to ¾ lb.
Loaf Sugar	2 to 6 ozs.	Stale Bread	2 rounds of loaf.

Put the sugar and water to boil. Prepare the fruit. Add it to the syrup. Simmer till soft. Cut the bread *very thinly and evenly.* Remove the crust. Line a basin with the bread. Place the basin on a plate. Pour the boiling fruit into the basin, but reserve a little of the syrup. Cover the fruit with a round of bread. Saturate this with syrup. Cover the pudding with another plate. Place a weight on the plate; when cold, turn out.

N.B.—The quantities stated are indefinite, as the yield varies with different fruits. The quantity of sugar and water must be in accordance with the fruit used. This pudding is most satisfactory when made with dark fruit, such as plums or blackberries, as then the bread is coloured and the juice surrounds the pudding as a finish. If apples or light coloured fruit are used, the following custard should be poured over it.

CUSTARD.

| Milk | ¼ pint. | Egg | 1. |
| Loaf Sugar | ½ oz. | | |

Heat the milk and dissolve the sugar in it. Beat the egg. Add it. Bring all to boiling point, but do not boil. Remove from fire, stir a few minutes. Cool and use.

Compôte of Oranges.

| Juicy Oranges | 6. | Water | 1 gill. |
| Cocoanut | 1 oz. | Loaf Sugar | 2 oz. |

Take the thin rind of one orange. Put it into an enamelled pan with the water and sugar. Boil gently to a nice thick syrup, about ten minutes, skimming it to keep it clear. Strain it and allow it to get cold. Peel all the oranges and take away every particle of the bitter white pith. Cut them in slices a quarter of an inch thick and take out the pips with a teaspoon. Arrange the slices in a glass dish, with layers of cocoanut in between. Pour the syrup over, and stand by an hour or so before serving. Tangerine oranges are nice for this dish. Sliced bananas may be used instead of the cocoa nut for garnish.

Boiled Custard (for Glasses).

Milk	½ pint.	Lemon Rind	1 strip.
Whole Egg	1	Castor Sugar	1½ oz.
Yolks	2		

Whisk the eggs in a basin lightly. Boil the milk and stir it a little at a time to the eggs, taking care not to curdle them. Strain into a jug. Add the lemon rind. Stand the jug in a pan of simmering water and stir until the custard thickens sufficiently to coat the back of the spoon. Take out of the water. Add the sugar, take out the lemon, and stir until the custard is cool, to prevent a scum forming on the top. Pour into custard glasses, and put two grates of nutmeg on top of each.

Apricot Mould.

| Apricots | 1 tin. | Castor Sugar | 3 ozs. |
| Cornflour | 1¾ ozs. | Cochineal | a few drops. |

Pass the apricots through a hair sieve. Add the sugar and cochineal, and stir to the boil in an enamel saucepan. Mix the cornflour into a smooth cream with cold water. Pour on the apricots. Stir well, return to the saucepan, and boil until quite clear, stirring well all the time. Turn into a wetted mould, and when cold turn out.

NOTE—These moulds can be done in the same way with any kind of fruit, or they may be set with ¼ oz. gelatine dissolved and stirred into the fruit.

CAKES.

Girdle Cakes.

Flour	¼ lb.	Currants	½ oz.
Baking Powder	¼ tspn.	Butter	2 ozs.
Salt	¼ tspn.	Water or milk.	

Put the girdle on to heat. Clean the currants. Sieve the flour, baking powder, and salt into a basin. Rub in the butter lightly with the tips of the fingers; leaving it in large pieces. The butter is left in large pieces to cause the flakes which are essential to girdle cakes. Drop in the currants, mix the paste as moist as it is possible when a rolling pin has to be used. Flour the board and pin. Roll out the mixture, fold and roll again very thinly (less than ¼ inch) it will rise in cooking. Cut round 2½ inches in diameter. Place them on the girdle. When lightly browned, turn, brown the second side lightly. When cooked the cakes should only be thick enough to split open. Split open and butter while warm.

Milk Rolls.

Vienna Flour	1 lb.	German Yeast	½ oz.
Salt	½ tspn.	Castor Sugar	½ tspn.
Butter	1½ oz.	Milk	½ pint.

Sieve the flour and salt. Rub the butter into the flour. Cream the yeast, and sugar. Warm the milk and add to the yeast; pour gradually into the centre of the flour and mix. Rise in a warm place one hour, knead well. Divide the dough into 12 pieces. Grease the tin; warm it. Put the rolls on; let them rise for ½ an hour. Bake in a quick oven about 20 minutes. When cooked rub over the top with butter.

Almond Cheese Cakes.

Short Crust	6 ozs.	White of Eggs	2½
Ground Almonds	2 ozs.	Water	1 dessertspn.
Almond Essence	2 drops.	Raspberry Jam.	
Castor Sugar	4 ozs.		

Line some greased patty-pans very thinly with the pastry, and place ½ teaspoonful of jam in the bottom of each. Mix castor sugar and ground almonds well together. Add essence to whites, and whisk stiffly, fold this quickly into the sugar, and add the water. Place sufficient mixture to cover jam in tartlets. Put on strips of pastry and bake in a hot oven 10 to 20 minutes.

Sally Luns.

Flour	½ lb.	Castor Sugar	¼ tspn.
Egg	1.	Butter	1 oz.
German Yeast	½ oz.	Lukewarm Milk	¼ pint.

Warm the basins. Sieve the flour and salt. Warm them. Cream the yeast, and sugar. Melt the butter in the milk. Pour a little of this on to the yeast and sugar. Add this to the centre of the flour. Beat the egg; pour it and the remainder of the milk into the flour. Beat all with the hand. Warm and grease 3 cake rings. Put in the dough. Cover. Rise 1½ hours. Start in a quick oven for 10 minutes. Bake in a moderate oven for 20 minutes.

PREPARE THE GLAZE.

Castor Sugar 1 tablespoon. | Milk 1 tablespoonful.

Mix sugar and milk. Brush it over and return the cakes to the oven for 2 minutes to dry.

Shortbread.

Flour	3 ozs.		Candied Peel	1 strip.
Butter	2 ozs.		Sugar	½ oz.

Sieve the flour; rub the butter in lightly. Work in the sugar with the hand. Flour the board. Mould the mixture on it into a round flat cake half-an-inch thick and five inches in diameter. Place on a baking sheet. Prick it all over. Pinch up the edges. Lay a strip of candied peel on the top. Bake in a moderate oven 30 to 40 minutes Let it remain on the sheet 5 minutes before moving it.

N.B.—The shortbread is improved by being allowed to stand a few hours before baking it.

Swiss Roll.

Flour	2 ozs.		Jam	2 tablespn.
Small Eggs	2.		Castor Sugar	2 ozs.
		Clarified Fat.		

Line the baking tin with paper, brush it very thoroughly with clarified fat. Sieve the flour on to paper. Break the eggs separately; if good, put them together in a basin. Sieve the sugar into these. Whisk till thick. Shake the flour in lightly. Mix it into the egg and sugar. Pour into the lined tin. Bake in a moderately quick oven for 7 minutes. Warm the jam. Dredge a paper with castor sugar. Test the roll with a skewer. If done, turn it out on to the paper. Remove the greased paper. Cut off the edges. Spread the jam, roll up. All this must be done quickly.

Cocoanut Buns.

Flour	½ lb.		Castor Sugar	4 oz.
Salt	a pinch.		Eggs	2.
Baking Powder	½ teaspn.		Dessicated Cocoanut	2 oz.
Butter	4 oz.		Milk	1 tblspn.

Grease the baking sheet. Cream the butter and sugar. Add the egg. Sieve the flour, salt and baking powder. Add these, the cocoanut, and milk by degrees. Drop on to the tin in small heaps. Bake 20 minutes in a moderate oven.

Fruit Cake.

Currants	1½ oz.	Salt	a pinch.
Raisins	1½ oz.	Castor Sugar	1½ oz.
Sultanas	1½ oz.	Butter	4 oz.
Peel	¾ oz.	Eggs	2.
Vienna Flour	8 ozs.	Oil for tin.	

Baking Powder ½ teaspoonful.

Prepare the paper for the cake tin. Reverse the tin, and place a piece of thick paper over the bottom. Press it well round the edges to get the size. Cut it the same size. Cut a band of paper, about three inches higher than the tin, and about 2 inches longer than the tin is round. Cut out darts on one edge of the band of paper. Brush the two pieces of paper over with oil. Line the sides of the tin. Place the round of paper on top of them. Wash the currants, dry, pick, and test them. Stone the raisins, cut them in halves. Flour the sultanas and remove stalks. Cut the peel. Sieve the flour. Cream the butter, add sugar, beat well; add the eggs, one at a time. Stir all well together. Stir in the dry ingredients. (If necessary add a little milk.) Mix well and put into prepared tin. Bake in a moderate oven for one hour. Do not turn it out immediately.

Shrewsbury Biscuits.

Butter	2 ozs.	Egg.	½
Castor Sugar	2 ozs.	Flour	¼ lb.

Lemon Rind ½.

Grease a baking sheet. Cream the butter and sugar. Add egg. Beat together. Sieve the flour and add lemon, and mix all into a paste. Flour a board; turn the paste on to it. Roll it out as thin as possible. Cut it into rounds 2½ inches in diameter. Place on tin. Bake in a moderate oven 20 minutes. The biscuits should be straw colour. Dry on sieve.

Sponge Cakes.

Flour	1 oz.	Egg	1.
Castor Sugar	1 oz.	Clarified fat to grease tins.	

Put the flour to dry. Grease 3 tins. Mix equal quantities (half teaspoonful) of castor sugar and flour. Dust it over the tins. Break the egg; if good add it to the sugar in a basin. Mix these. Beat over warm water for about ten minutes. Sieve the flour to the egg and sugar. Stir as little and as lightly as possible. Pour into the prepared tins. Bake in a moderate oven 20 minutes. When firm on the top they are done. Do not remove them from the tins for a few minutes after they are taken from the oven.

Eccles Cakes.

6 ozs. Flaky Pastry or Rough Puff Pastry (see page 60).

MIXTURE.

Currants	2 ozs.	Allspice	$\frac{1}{4}$ teaspoonful.
Sugar	1 oz.	Nutmeg	a little grated.
Peel	$\frac{3}{4}$ oz.	Butter	$\frac{1}{2}$ oz.

Roll out the paste, cut into rounds, place in the centre 2 teaspoonfuls of the mixture. Close up the rounds, flatten with a rolling pin, mark across the top of each cake with a knife, brush over with white of egg, sprinkle on castor sugar, bake in a quick oven 10 to 15 minutes.

For the mixture cream the butter and sugar, add the currants (washed), the peel (chopped), sugar, spice and butter. Mix them altogether, and use as directed above.

Soda Cake.

Flour	1 lb.	Currants	$\frac{1}{4}$ lb.
Butter	$\frac{1}{2}$ lb.	Sultanas	$\frac{1}{4}$ lb.
Sugar	$\frac{1}{2}$ lb.	Raisins	$\frac{1}{4}$ lb.
Salt	$\frac{1}{2}$ teaspoon.	Peel	$\frac{1}{4}$ lb.
Nutmeg or Mixed Spice		Eggs	2.
	1 teaspoon.	Milk	$\frac{1}{4}$ pint.

Carbonate of Soda, 1 teaspoonful.

Rub butter into flour, add all dry ingredients except soda. Slightly beat eggs, dissolve soda in milk; add both to mixture, beat well for about 5 minutes, pour into greased tin, and bake in moderate oven about $1\frac{3}{4}$ hours.

Drop Scones.

Flour	3 ozs.	Sugar	$\frac{3}{4}$ oz.
Soda	$\frac{1}{2}$ teaspoonful.	Cream of Tartar	$\frac{1}{2}$ teaspoonful
Egg	$\frac{1}{2}$.	Pinch of Salt.	

Milk $\frac{1}{2}$ gill.

Mix flour, salt and sugar together, add egg and sufficient milk to make a thick batter. Beat well, add cream of tartar and cream of soda (dry), stir quickly in. Drop on very hot girdle, when set on under side, turn with a palette knife. Brown on both sides. Cook for about $1\frac{1}{2}$ to 2 minutes.

Madeira Cake.

Flour	8 ozs.	Eggs	3.
Baking Powder	½ teaspoonful.	Citron	3 slices.
Butter	4 ozs.	Lemon	½ rind grated.
Sugar	4 ozs.	Milk	1 tablespoonful.

Cream the butter and sugar till white, add the eggs, one at a time, and beat well. Lightly stir in the flour and baking powder previously sieved, also the grated lemon rind, add the milk, pour into prepared tin, place the citron on the top. Bake in a moderate oven 1 hour.

Queen Cakes.

Flour	3 ozs.	Cherries	4.
Butter	2 ozs.	Lemon	½ rind grated.
Sugar	2 ozs.	Baking Powder	¼ teaspoonful.
Candied Peel	1 oz.	Egg	1 large.
Sultanas	2 ozs.	Milk	1 tablespnful.

Grease 8 queen cake tins. Clean the sultanas. Shred the candied peel, cut the cherries into quarters. Pass the flour, baking powder, and a pinch of salt through a sieve, and grate on to it the lemon rind. Cream the butter and sugar until quite white, beat in the egg, add the milk, lightly stir in the flour, add the fruit, put the mixture into the tins, and bake in a moderate oven about 20 minutes.

Lunch Cake.

Flour	½ lb.	Peel	1½ ozs.
Butter	¼ lb.	Lemon	½ rind, grated
Sugar	¼ lb.	Baking Powder	½ teaspn.
Sultanas	2 ozs.	Eggs	1.
Currants	2 ozs.	Milk	¾ gill.

Rub the butter into the flour, add the prepared fruit. Beat the egg with the milk. Mix quickly, pour into prepared tin and bake in a moderate oven for 1 hour.

Brandy Snaps.

Butter	2 ozs.	Golden Syrup	2 ozs.
Sugar	2 ozs.	Ground Ginger	½ teaspn.
Flour	2 ozs.		

Melt the butter, sugar, and syrup in a pan, then add the ginger and flour and stir well till properly mixed.

Grease a baking sheet. Drop on a teaspoonful of the mixture at intervals. Bake in slow oven until brown. When slightly cold turn over the handle of a wooden spoon. They may be filled with whipped cream, flavoured with vanilla and sweetened.

PASTRY.

Cheese Straws.

Cheddar Cheese	1 oz.	Cayenne and Salt.	
Parmesan Cheese	2 ozs.	Egg Yolk	1.
Flour	2 ozs.	Water	2 teaspful.
Butter	2 ozs.		

Grate the cheese. Rub the butter into the flour. Add salt, cayenne, and cheese. Mix to a stiff paste with the yolk of egg and water. Roll out; cut into strips 4 inches long and quarter inch wide. Place on a baking sheet. Bake in a slow oven about 15 minutes. Dish in rows, crosswise, or in bundles.

Lemon Cheesecakes.

Flour	4 ozs.	Lard	$1\frac{1}{2}$ ozs.
Salt	a pinch.	Water.	
Butter	$1\frac{1}{2}$ ozs.	Lemon Juice	$\frac{1}{2}$ teaspoonful.

Rub the flour and salt through a sieve. Cut the butter and lard into small pieces; mix these into the flour, keep them in lumps. Add lemon juice and water to form the paste. Flour board and pin; roll out the paste with a short forward push till it becomes long, thin, and narrow; fold in three; keep the edges even; press them with the pin; turn the smooth edges to the right hand. Roll out as before and fold. Put aside to get cold.

PREPARE THE LEMON CHEESE.

Loaf Sugar	$\frac{1}{4}$ lb.	Egg	1.
Lemon	1.	Butter	2 ozs.

Wipe the lemon, rub the sugar on the rind, and put it in an enamelled saucepan. Squeeze out the juice, strain it over sugar. Add butter; melt over the fire; cool. Beat the egg, and add. Stir over the fire until the mixture coats the spoon; do not let it boil.

This mixture can be made in a jar surrounded by boiling water.

Roll and fold the pastry for another 3 turns (5 in all). The pastry should become smooth and elastic. Cut out rounds and fit them into patty-pans. Prick the bottom and fill with the mixture. Bake in a very quick oven for 15 minutes.

Raised Pie.

Lard	1½ oz.	Lean Meat	4 ozs.
Milk	3 tablespoons.	Salt.	
Flour	3 ozs.	Water	1 tablespoon.

Melt lard in four tablespoons of water and boil up. Pour into flour; mix and leave in a warm place. Cut the meat off the bones. Cover bones with cold water in a small saucepan. Add a little salt. Simmer to make stock for the pie. Cut the meat up small and season it. Sprinkle with one tablespoonful of water. Cut off a small piece of dough for the top. Keep it warm. Work the rest of the dough smooth. Mould it quickly into the shape of a drum or round box. Pack the meat in, wet the edges. Roll out the top, put it on, make a hole in the top. Trim and decorate and glaze with egg. Bake one hour in a slow oven. When done, put the stock in through the hole at the top.

Short Crust.

Flour	½ lb.	Baking Powder	¼ teaspn.
Butter or Lard	¼ lb.	Sugar	½ teaspn.

Pass flour and baking powder through a sieve into a basin. Rub in the butter or lard, very lightly, until the mixture resembles fine bread crumbs; add sugar; mix in sufficient very cold water to make into a stiff paste (about quarter pint). This must be done as quickly and lightly as possible. Roll out at once and use. If wanted for meat dishes leave out the sugar and use salt.

Welsh Cheesecakes.

Pastry	¼ lb. or trimmings.	Sugar ⎫	
Jam	2 tablespoonfuls.	Butter ⎬ Weight of egg.	
Egg	1.	Flour ⎭	
		Baking Powder	¼ teaspoonful.
		Lemon	½ rind grated.

Line patty-pans thinly with the pastry, put into each a little jam, and above that 1 teaspoonful of cheese-cake mixture. Bake in a quick oven for 15 minutes. Sprinkle over with castor sugar before serving.

CHEESE CAKE MIXTURE.

Cream, butter, and sugar together until quite white, add the egg, and stir the flour and grated lemon rind lightly in.

Rough Puff Pastry.

Flour	8 ozs.	Lemon Juice,	½ teaspoonful.
Butter or Lard,	6 ozs.	Salt	¼ teaspoonful.

Put the flour and salt through a sieve into a basin. Cut the butter or lard into pieces about the size of a walnut and mix into the flour. Make a hole in the centre, pour in the lemon juice and sufficient cold water to mix into a stiff paste. Mix very lightly, and try not to break the pieces of butter. Turn on to a floured paste board, and roll out to a long narrow strip. Fold in three and roll again. Repeat this until you have given the pastry four rolls and folds. Keep in a cool place until wanted. This pastry is used for meat pies, sausage rolls, mince pies, &c.

Flaky Pastry.

Flour	9 ozs.	Pinch of Salt.
Lard	3 ozs.	Cold Water.
Butter	3 ozs.	

Pass the flour through a sieve into a bowl. Take half the fat and rub it lightly into the flour with the tips of the fingers, keeping the flour as cool as possible. Add the salt, and mix into a stiff paste with cold water (the less water used the better, so long as the paste is not made tough). Rub a little flour on the board and on the rolling pin. Roll the pastry into a long strip, square at the edges, about an eighth-of-an-inch thick. Divide the other half of the fat into three; lay one part in little pieces all down the crust evenly; dust slightly with flour; fold the crust into three; give it one turn round, so that the open flap of pastry is at your right hand; seal the edges to keep in the air, and roll out the same thickness again, commencing from the middle, so as to disperse the air in tiny bubbles all over the crust. Proceed in this way until all the fat is rolled in, and if it is not thoroughly mixed with three rolls, give it one or even two rolls without any fat, always folding into three.

INVALID COOKERY.

Cup of Cornflour or Arrowroot.

Cornflour or Arrowroot ½ oz		Milk	½ pint.
	Loaf Sugar	¼ oz.	

Mix the cornflour with a tablespoonful of cold milk. Put the remainder of the milk in a saucepan to boil. Add the sugar. Pour the cornflour into the milk. Stir quickly, and boil till it thickens. Pour into a cup.

Cornflour or Arrowroot Pudding.

| Cup of Cornflour, as above. | Egg | 1. |
| Butter | 1 oz. | Castor Sugar | $\frac{1}{4}$ oz. |

Grease a pie dish with butter. Turn the cup of cornflour into a basin. Separate the yolk and white of egg. Beat the yolk and sugar into the cornflour. Whip the white up stiffly. Add it lightly. Pour the mixture into the pie dish. Bake 15 minutes in a moderate oven.

Egg Jelly.

Gelatine	$\frac{1}{4}$ oz.	Loaf Sugar	3 ozs.
Water	$\frac{1}{4}$ pint.	Lemon Juice & Water	$\frac{1}{4}$ pint.
Lemon	1.	Egg	1.

Fill the mould with cold water. Soak the gelatine in a quarter pint of water. Rub the sugar on the lemon. Put sugar, water, and gelatine over the fire to dissolve. Squeeze out the juice of the lemon. Make up quarter pint of liquid with water. Add this to the saucepan and remove from the fire. Separate the yolk and white of the egg, beat the yolk, and add to the pan. Put this over the fire. Bring to the boiling point to set the egg. Whip the white to a stiff froth. Stir it in lightly. Turn the water out of the mould. Pour the mixture in. Stand till cold. Turn out.

In summer use more gelatine. If preferred, the egg need not be separated, but used whole.

NOTE:—Metal spoons or pans will discolour the jelly.

Irish Moss Jelly.

Irish Moss	$\frac{1}{4}$ oz.	Milk	1 pint.
Cold Water.		Lemon Rind	2 strips.
	Loaf Sugar, 1 oz.		

Put the moss to soak in cold water for 10 or 12 hours. Change the water. Drain the moss. Pick away any impurities or coloured pieces. Put it into a saucepan with the milk and the lemon rind. Let it come slowly to the boil. Simmer gently for 1 hour, or until the moss is dissolved. Add the sugar. Strain into a wet mould. When cold, turn out.

Rice and Apple Snow.

Large Apples	2.	Egg	1.
Milk	½ pint.	Butter	¼ oz.
Lemon Rind	a strip.	Castor Sugar	1 or 1½ oz.
Loaf Sugar	½ oz.	Lemon Juice	few drops.
Ground Rice	1½ oz.	Pink Sugar	1 tspn.

Wipe the apples, prick them, and place on a tin in a moderate oven for 20 or 30 minutes. Fill two pie cups with cold water. Put the lemon rind in the milk, make it hot. Dissolve the sugar in it, and remove the rind. Sprinkle in the ground rice. Simmer till the milk is absorbed by the rice. Separate the yolk and white of the egg. Beat the yolk, mix it carefully into the saucepan. Add butter. Heat the mixture, but do not let it boil. Turn the water from the pie cups, pour in the rice mixture. Rub the apple through a hair sieve; beat well. Whip the white of egg stiffly. Sweeten, and add lemon juice. Beat the egg white and apple together till they are white and firm. When the rice is cold turn the shapes on to separate plates. Pile the apple snow over each one. Serve *at once*.

Egg Flip.

Egg	1.	Sugar	1 dessertspoonful.
		Brandy,	¼ glass.

Stir the raw yolk of egg and sugar together in a tumbler until creamy. Add the wine. Whip the white of egg to a stiff froth and lightly stir in.

Chicken Panade.

Chicken or Veal	½ lb.	Cream	½ gill.
	Pepper and Salt.		

Mince the veal or chicken finely, place in a well buttered jar or jampot, cover with a greased paper, place in boiling water, cook gently for 1 hour. Pound the meat in a mortar and rub with the liquid through a wire sieve. Whip the cream slightly, stir in the meat, season, serve hot or cold on dry toast or in ramakins.

Chicken Broth.

Chicken	1.	Water	1 qt.
Mace	1 blade.	Rice or Barley	1 oz.
Parsley, chopped	1 dessrtspnfl.	Salt	1 teaspoonful.
	Onion, 1 small.		

Cut off the breast and meat from the wings; these will do for another dish. Cut up the rest of the chicken into small joints and put with bones into a saucepan, add the cold water and salt and bring to the boil, draw off the fire and skim, cut the onion into slices, wash the rice, and put into the saucepan with mace and simmer gently for two hours. Take out all the bones and mace, put the parsley into a tureen and pour the broth over, or the broth can all be passed through a hair sieve and a little milk added. If there is any chicken fat floating on the broth, remove it with kitchen paper.

Mutton Broth.

Mutton, middle neck of 1 lb.	Parsley	1 sprig.
Water	1½ pts.	Rice	½ oz.
	Salt.		

Remove fat and marrow from meat, and cut into small joints, put into saucepan with salt and water, and bring slowly to the boil; take off the fire and skim off all scum, add the rice and a little onion if allowed, and simmer gently for 2 hours; take out the meat and remove all traces of fat. Serve with a little finely chopped parsley, in a cup.

Furniture Polish
2 oz Bees Wax
1 — White —
½ oz Castile soap
1 Pt Turpentine
Grate wax and cover with
Turpentine cut up soap
and pour a gill of
boiling water over it —
let it stand 24 hrs
mix well together
bottle for use

Cough Mixture
½ lb Treacle
3 tablespoons Vinegar & Rum
2 small Teaspoonfull of
~~Laud~~ m Laudanum
Mix well together

This book is a photographic facsimile of an original copy. It is
doubtful whether more than one or two originals now exist and
our copy, **101** years old, fell apart while being scanned. It included the two
handwritten recipes shown on the preceding page, which are as follows:

Furniture Polish

2 oz Bees wax
1 oz White wax
½ oz Castile soap
1 pt turpentine

Grate wax and cover with turpentine, cut up soap, [add to the mixture]
and pour a gill of boiling water over it.
Let it stand 24 hours; mix well together.
Bottle for use.

Cough mixture

½ lb treacle
3 tablespoons vinegar and rum
2 small teaspoonsful of Laudanum

Mix well together

Note: the recipe is not clear whether it needs 3 tablespoons each of
vinegar and rum, or 3 spoons of an equal mix ...
due to the inclusion of laudanum, this is no longer a recommended
home made remedy.

Diversions Books
April 28. 2014

Milton Keynes UK
Ingram Content Group UK Ltd.
UKHW031316260824
1386UKWH00016B/74